palgrave▶**pivot**

What Has the Black Church to Do with Public Life?

Anthony B. Pinn

palgrave
macmillan

DOI: 10.1057/9781137376954

WHAT HAS THE BLACK CHURCH TO DO WITH PUBLIC LIFE?
Copyright © Anthony B. Pinn, 2013.

First published in 2013 by
PALGRAVE MACMILLAN®
in the United States—a division of St. Martin's Press LLC,
175 Fifth Avenue, New York, NY 10010.

Where this book is distributed in the UK, Europe and the rest of the world,
this is by Palgrave Macmillan, a division of Macmillan Publishers Limited,
registered in England, company number 785998, of Houndmills,
Basingstoke, Hampshire RG21 6XS.

Palgrave Macmillan is the global academic imprint of the above companies
and has companies and representatives throughout the world.

Palgrave® and Macmillan® are registered trademarks in the United States,
the United Kingdom, Europe and other countries.

ISBN: 978-1-137-37696-1 EPUB
ISBN: 978-1-137-37695-4 PDF
ISBN: 978-1-137-38050-0 Hardback

Library of Congress Cataloging-in-Publication Data is available from the
Library of Congress.

A catalogue record of the book is available from the British Library.

First edition: 2013

www.palgrave.com/pivot

DOI: 10.1057/9781137376954

Contents

Preface

Abstract: *We have reached a point in conversation concerning the intersection of religious life and the public arena that requires attention to the proper role of religion within public life. Assumptions have been made concerning this role, but questions remain. This preface outlines my rationale for undertaking the presentation of this manifesto as well as my concern to use the Black church as a case study for exploring the role in public life of theism in more general terms.*

▶

According to numerous studies, the majority of African Americans believe in God, and the large number of independent and denominational black churches spread across the United States suggests many of these believers express this belief institutionally. In these churches some believers spend Sundays worshipping God. They then apply teachings regarding this God to mundane life over the remainder of the week. This is the typically told story of African American religious expression—black churches shaping the private attitudes and practices of the faithful. Few debate this narrative. More controversial and less easily captured, however, is the actual public profile of black churches.

By public profile, I am not referencing private indiscretions of ministers announced on CNN, Fox News, local evening news shows, or one of the other television, radio, or social media outlets. These episodes challenge the chosen-ness or special-ness of religious leaders and expose the holes in their "privileged" ethical status. In a more

DOI: 10.1057/9781137376954

general sense, episodes of moral failure make easy targets of not only church leadership but also church members who do not practice what they proclaim. These embarrassing episodes come along more often than churches might like (to admit), and they require theological damage control and ritual slight-of-hand. But these moments of theological spin aren't the concern guiding this book.

Nor do I mean by public profile efforts to evangelize beyond the walls of church buildings by taking the Gospel into ordinary spaces of life—street corners, parks, and stadiums. Instead, I have in mind involvement of black churches in public issues and debates—black churches attempting to influence policy and other markers of collective, public life, arranged within what we have come to label the public arena.

Numerous scholars and much of the general public familiar with black churches have assumed these institutions played a significant and indisputable role in not simply the survival but the private-public advancement of African American peoples. And while there is no doubt that many, but certainly not all, black churches have placed themselves into public life, the question of whether there has been benefit to this remains alive and requires attention.

The Black church—by which is meant the matrix of African American Christian churches, denominations, fellowships, and communions—has received a great deal of attention in both scholarship and popular outlets. W. E. B. Du Bois, Anna J. Cooper, Carter G. Woodson, Benjamin Mays, E. Franklin Frazier, C. Eric Lincoln, and others have described and analyzed its nature and meaning as the first institution created for and by African Americans. For a good number of years now, it has been a central symbol of African American organizational creativity and broad thought—producing and spreading a meta-narrative of productive struggle for a deep sense of humanity.

Even when it is critiqued, more often than not, the frustration expressed results from a feeling that the Black church should and can do better and do more to help African Americans.

My concern is the appropriateness and usefulness of such activities on the part of churches. The removal of the qualifier in the previous sentence— *"Black"—is intentional in that, while my discussion in this slim volume is limited to black churches, I believe the question raised here should inform understandings of all institutionalized religion within public discourse in more general terms (even when these religions are perceived as being humanistic).*

DOI: 10.1057/9781137376954

Mindful of this agenda, my attention to black churches is a case study, an example of how this discussion of religion in the public arena might go. In terms of my rationale, I use black churches as a case study because of the general assumption within US popular thought that black churches are, and have always been, the mainstay of black communities. That is to say, for many within the United States, black churches serve as an exemplar of religious engagement with public life. Hence, why not begin a discussion of the utility of religion in the public arena with what is considered a prime example of this type of involvement?

But, really, what should the Black church do in the public sphere? Does the presence of black churches—think in terms of the "influence" of their theological posture informing public perception of socio-political issues—hamper or help the health of public debate and progress? Are black churches the best (or even a reliable) mechanism for shaping public thought and policy, and, by extension, for distributing public resources? Simply put, should black churches play a role in shaping the public arena and the public life of African Americans?

Many who respond in the affirmative to such questions do so because they frame the challenges facing African American communities as stemming from various moral failures, and they promote black churches as *the* institutions best prepared to address moral- and value-driven problems. Others respond in the affirmative because of how they read mid-twentieth century civil rights gains as having been dependent on the will and bodies of African American Christians, as well as the resources of the churches housing them.

Still others, like me, are more cautious in their celebration of "Black church" involvements in the public arena—arguing instead that churches are best equipped to manage the private, spiritual needs of those who claim membership in them.

Because this third response is less firmly lodged in traditional perceptions of black church life, it requires the attention I give it here—beginning with a rehearsal of particular historical developments but with an eye on what these developments have meant regarding black churches' perception of their public responsibilities and capacities.

This point is vital: my presentation of black church activism does not contradict the purpose of this volume. It is not my opinion that black churches—and other religious organizations—have not been involved in public life. So, the presentation of such efforts on their part doesn't negate my claim. Rather, I raise questions concerning common misperceptions

DOI: 10.1057/9781137376954

of what this involvement means as well as the long range value of such involvement. And, I use these examples of church involvement with public issues to highlight and isolate the internal arrangements, structures, and thought patterns of these churches that prevent them from having an ultimately productive and useful place in public discourse.

In taking this approach, my goal is not to close churches—or other religious organizations—nor is it to promote an uninformed secularism, but rather to encourage public life in which all institutions (religious and atheistic) do as little harm as possible to public health and well-being in a changing population. This outcome requires rigorous and sustained debate in line with the best elements of a democratic process. For such debate to take place in its most productive forms there needs to be a general dismissal of religious organizations as having an unchallenged and special place within US life—a location in collective life that exempts them from the need for transparency of aims and conduct.

I want to make clear that this book is not simply "New Atheism" vitriol against all religion (typically meaning religious fundamentalism of all stripes) in all spaces of life. In fact, many of my atheist colleagues might find this text much too accommodating, too concerned with collaborations that can't be grounded in the dominance of reason and science. Many within the "New Atheism" camp—those with a particularly aggressive read of the "separation of church and state," for example, might dismiss this text as useless pandering to the religious. I disagree.

I seek to provide something much more nuanced, and something more mindful of the historical development and context of black church involvement—all the time being aware that *both* theistic and nontheistic fundamentalisms truncate possibilities for a transformative public arena. And, I set out this agenda as someone who has been in the church and now is a nontheistic humanist who studies seriously African American religions in particular and religion in America in more general terms.

Finally, it is important to point out that this volume is meant as a manifesto, and by that I mean a statement of my view, of my opinion. Furthermore, it is prescriptive in that it provides suggestions concerning a new approach to religion in the public arena. In addition, it is tied to, and helps to clarify, my earlier work related to the nature and meaning of black religion and my interrogation of nontheistic humanism.

DOI: 10.1057/9781137376954

The goal of this manifesto is to provide some context for understanding the relationship of African American Christianity in the form of black churches to public life—the intersections of morality, politics, and religion as ethicist Peter Paris labels the three pillars of African American church reality—and to assess this connection.[1] Ultimately, it uses this discussion as a launching point for suggesting, in dialogue with a progressive religionist, a framing of discourse on issues of policy that appreciates private religiosity and the secular nature of the public arena.

Note

1   For Peter Paris' thought see, for example, *The Spirituality of African Peoples* (Minneapolis: Fortress Press, 2008).

DOI: 10.1057/9781137376954

Acknowledgments

Formal presentations and conversations with a variety of people ground this short book. Friends within the academy as well as those within various humanist and atheist organizations provided opportunities for me to present my ideas as well as food for thought that inform my thinking on this important topic. While we didn't always agree on the particulars of the topic, what they offered in our exchanges was invaluable. I thank them all for their challenges and insights, patience in listening to my perspective, and for good humor and deep concern for the intersections of religion and public life. I hope they find in these pages a clear indication of my regard for their thought and the topic. I must also thank my student, Christopher Driscoll, for his assistance with preparing the manuscript for delivery to the press. R. Drew Smith was kind enough to read and comment on a shorter version of this project, and I am grateful for his insights and suggestions. Finally, I owe a debt of gratitude to Rabbi Michael Lerner for the invitation to write a piece—"The Problem with Black Churches in the Public Arena"—for *Tikkun Daily* (*tikkun.org/daily*, March 11, 2013). This volume is an extension of that article, and some of the questions he posed in an email exchange we had regarding the focus of that particular piece.

DOI: 10.1057/9781137376954

palgrave▶pivot

www.palgrave.com/pivot

1

Early Efforts to Be Black and Christian in Public

Abstract: *This chapter explores the effort of black churches to shape the public presentation of African Americans in ways that would present African Americans as "acceptable" and consistent with existing socio-political standards for citizenship. In this way, it points out the activities that gave rise to the assumption that black churches are the best means by which to address the public needs and desires of African Americans. The period covered in this chapter extends to Reconstruction.*

Pinn, Anthony B. *What Has the Black Church to Do with Public Life?* New York: Palgrave Macmillan, 2013.
DOI: 10.1057/9781137376954.

In 1842, a former slave from Raleigh, North Carolina, received assistance in writing a letter to a small paper in Brooklyn, New York. In the letter, he outlined the details of his financial effort to purchase his freedom and that of his family—wife and children. What is rather intriguing about the letter is the importance he places on membership in the Methodist Episcopal Church, and this is accompanied by a rather nebulous recognition of assistance received. "They," the letter remarks, "earnestly thank God for thus answering their prayers, compassionating them in their distress, and crowning their efforts with the desired prosperity..."[1] This framing of church participation and the outcomes of such involvement in religious life and religious community is a common sentiment within early African American communities.

For example, some years prior to the above statement being written, Richard Allen, the first bishop of the African Methodist Episcopal Church, outlined the significance of church membership with respect to more than spiritual renewal. He noted the capacity of these churches to inform and influence both the private—health of the soul—and public dimensions of individual and collective life. By that he meant black churches held the capacity to improve the spiritual well-being of people of African descent as well as to foster within them the traits and characteristics, the moral and ethical postures, necessary for their efforts to secure physical freedom and full participation in the life of the Nation.

In this way, church buildings were to serve a variety of purposes: locations for preaching the gospel, spaces of spiritual fellowship, places for the nurturing of morality and discipline, and sites for the advancement of social sensibilities. These three taken together—proper knowledge, spiritual well-being, and proper conduct—would ultimately, Allen and others believed, push the larger society to embrace African Americans as equals with full rights and responsibilities. This is not to say Allen and others associated with early black churches believed that people of African descent were depraved and inferior in any inherent way. To the contrary, they understood the manner in which the system of slavery and racial discrimination limited opportunities for moral and ethical conduct and forced the refining of the worst traits in both white colonists and people of African descent. One key target in correcting this predicament involved the manner in which anti-black racism challenged private relationships, with wide implications.

DOI: 10.1057/9781137376954

Morality and public life

As part of this religiously fueled reconstitution of individuals and communities, many African American church leaders gave attention to the proper structuring and management of families. The "cult of true womanhood" and theory of domesticity were praised as a posture toward the world and philosophy of family whereby women were relegated to home as the proper arena for their influence and men to the public spheres of life. The formation of familial relationships was of deep importance to enslaved Africans in North America, and they worked to foster such relationships to the best of their ability and within the strictures of the slave system. However, churches provided a space in which this effort was affirmed and where theological and ritual structures were in place to enhance the value of this effort.

This familial arrangement in line with dominate perceptions of gender and social roles required a moral and ethical base, in the case of African Americans, an exorcising of the worst life habits encouraged by enslavement and anti-black racism. Therefore, reasonable and productive life in relationship to others—both publicly and in the privacy of one's family and friends—demanded possession of a moral compass and ethical posture toward the world consistent with the best teachings of the Christian faith and expressed in the doctrine and practices of the Christian churches. In short, many of these earlier churches took upon themselves a public ministry revolving around moral reform and sociopolitical activism (to the extent circumstances allowed). It was understood churches needed to be both physical space and intellectual space offering mechanisms for advancing educational skills, social talents and capacities, as well as shaping opinions on public issues such as abolition and democratic vision.

White preachers and Christian slaveholders often advanced the need for modesty and conservative conduct, but that was meant to safeguard the structures of enslavement. In opposition to this conformist thinking, for Richard Allen and others like him, moral reform was intended to serve as a force against enslavement and socio-political marginality. And, through religious services, gatherings, and sermons, proper moral conduct was described and practiced as a model for approaches to life outside the sanctity of worship. With no access to the written word because of laws against teaching enslaved Africans to read and write,

DOI: 10.1057/9781137376954

performance and modeling of conduct as a lived expression of religious doctrine and creeds had to take precedence over written codes of morality and ethics.

The sermon became a prime opportunity to expound the virtues of the Christian faith and the manner in which it targets and corrects immoral and unethical behavior. What is more, the Christian faith was assumed able to challenge groups to live out the best elements of their character. George Liele, who would become an important Baptist minister, recounted the way in which a sermon convicted him and pointed to his moral defects: "The Rev. Mr. Matthew Moore, one Sabbath afternoon, as I stood with curiosity to hear him," Liele reflects, "unfolded all my dark views, opened my best behaviour and good works to me, which I thought I was to be saved by, and I was convinced that I was not in the way to heaven, but in the way to hell."[2]

Religion, in general, and churches in particular were believed to have the vision, capacity, and commitment to point out these deficiencies in white colonists and people of African descent. Hence, early black church leaders understood the necessity of critiquing and correcting the practices and attitudes within communities of both whites and blacks. For instance, the hypocrisy of Christian claims by those very persons supporting the system of slavery was not lost on African American Christians—who critiqued this moral and ethical failure and proposed an alternate approach to individual and collective life. Whites, these churches and church leaders argued, must dismantle socio-economic and political structures that require and feed on the dehumanization of people of African descent; and, the latter must refine the traits and capacities necessary for full and productive participation in the life of the United States. Added to this was recognition that these black churches—despite some opposition and push back from whites and white denominations—in most cases, were the only spaces in which African Americans felt a significant degree of ownership over their time and intent, spaces where their own desires and needs guided their agendas. Many have argued that it was within these religious spaces where people of African descent knew their humanity; their worth was assumed to be in place and of deep significance. This recognition of human agency might have inspired blacks, but it raised concerns for whites interested in maintaining the status quo.

DOI: 10.1057/9781137376954

A morality tale at work

Resistance by whites due to fear that religious freedom might promote a desire for physical freedom and equality, combined with verification of this fear through religiously inspired and fueled slave revolts meant limited access to enslaved African Americans on plantations in the South and great difficulty for enslaved and free African Americans in the North. Yet, the number of African American Baptists and Methodists grew in both independent African American churches and white-led churches as a consequence of the first Great Awakening (1730s–1740s) and the second Great Awakening (roughly 1790s–1860s).

Targeting different regions of the nation, these spiritual revivals brought large numbers of people into churches that expressed their spiritual commitments with energy. For example, according to historian Albert Raboteau, prior to the development of the African Methodist Episcopal Church denomination, the Methodist Episcopal denomination claimed roughly 11,600 African American members in 1790. Less than a decade later, the number was over 12,215—representing roughly one-fourth the total Methodist membership. Some estimates put the number of African American Baptists at 18,000 by 1793. And the number would increase to 40,000 by 1813.[3]

In addition to influential local churches, the nineteenth century also ushered in the development of more advanced African American religious organizational structures. More to the point, the effectiveness of black churches in spreading the story of their purpose and importance is marked most graphically by the growth experienced by independent African American denominations—with hierarchies and structures pushing beyond localized demographics—before the end of the nineteenth century. For example, African American Methodists developed denominations that covered numerous states. Furthermore, African American Baptists began developing regional associations—e.g., Providence Association in Ohio (1834) and the Wood River Association in Illinois (1839)[4]—meant to better utilize limited resources in ways that maximized potential for executing public agendas related to moral and political advancement. These regional associations would eventually give rise to national Baptist conventions, starting in 1895 with the National Baptist Convention, USA.

Based, to some degree, on these and other structural developments, many African Americans found church a place to address a variety

DOI: 10.1057/9781137376954

of life circumstances and concerns. Ministers often encouraged this expansive approach to church responsibility and obligation through sermons as well as programs meant to address the enhancement of character and transformation of the socio-political workings of the Nation.

Church activities and thought generally reflected optimism regarding the potential of the United States to live out its most profound principles as well as hammered home the value of hard work and moral correctness as means by which to secure full participation in the inner workings of public life. In essence, this strategy was three pronged: (1) critique and corrective to the patterns of discrimination impacting African Americans; (2) promotion in African Americans of the characteristics, sensibilities, and moral outlook believed necessary for full citizenship; (3) advancement of organizational structures meant to shape and promote churches' public agenda.

Some African American Christians found this approach too slow-moving and without the desired effect. As an alternate approach, slave revolts—while maintaining a Christian ethos—spoke forcefully to a critique and corrective of discriminatory patterns. According to historian Gayraud Wilmore, revolts of varying size took place in noteworthy quantities after 1800 in the South. Methodist Denmark Vesey and Baptist Nat Turner led two of the most (in)famous of these revolts. Vesey's took place in 1822, and it was rumored that the African Methodist Episcopal Church played some role in the plot, with one of the denomination's ministers—Morris Brown—providing advice and aid. Turner understood his 1831 revolt as a mission consistent with religious ministry and demanded by his faith's call to righteousness. Although the damage done by such revolts was minimal, they loomed large in the popular imagination of citizens and pointed to the synergy between religious commitment and public protest.

While figures such as Maria Stewart (the first African American woman to lecture publicly on political issues—Boston, 1831) utilized this style of rhetoric, the slave revolts presented—in word and deed—the most graphic Jeremiad in that they gave physical form to the demand for justice as the only means by which to avoid destruction and judgment. Morality and ethics were linked by the Jeremiad (based on the proclamations made by the Hebrew Bible prophet Jeremiah) through a justice/advancement and injustice/destruction motif. Tied to this Jeremiad was often a sense of chosen-ness, a special place and status for African

DOI: 10.1057/9781137376954

Americans in that they are God's people who will be freed from bondage. However, it spoke also more generally to loyalty "both to the principles of egalitarian liberalism and to the Anglo-Christian code of values." In light of the demands of God concerning human conduct, anti-black racism violated both natural and divine law.[5]

In addition to actions on the part of African Americans and their supporters, church members and leaders provided more coded critiques and correctives in sermons and through the ritual structures of their churches. For example, sermons—even when whites were present— often spoke to a need for moral correctness consistent with the ministry of Jesus the Christ. That is, these sermons often called out hypocrisy: the practices of the larger society did not jibe with the demands of the faith its supporters claimed. Furthermore, it was understood this critique could not be one directional in nature.

Black churches also had an obligation to equip African American Christians with the tools necessary for spiritual health and physical well-being in the existential spheres of public life. For instance, fueled with spiritual warning, Richard Allen's attention to moral reform meant a warning to young men to avoid bad examples. "Drunkenness hurls reason from the throne, and when she has fallen," he announces, "Vice stands ready to ascent it. Break off, O young man your impious companions. If you still grasp their hands they will drag you down to everlasting fire."[6] Such advice had its most sustained impact on individual Christians seeking spiritual advancement, but it was the societies and other substructures of black churches that addressed public life and moral reform on a collective level. In short, many assumed a strong connection between morality and abolition, and churches developed strategies in light of this assumption. Associated with African American Methodists in Philadelphia, James Forten and Absalom Jones created in 1809 an organization named the "Society for the Suppression of Vice and Immorality" intended as the pedagogical arm of the Church. The organization attacked the vice noted by Allen in the quotation above— alcohol use—believing that such an attack would destroy one excuse used to deny African Americans political opportunities and involvement.[7] They would help to foster the formation of strong character free of alcoholism and thus end the assumption that African American abuse of strong drink prevented them from being equipped to participate in the public life of the Nation.[8] It was also understood that this approach to morality had to be coupled with attention to other social skills, job

DOI: 10.1057/9781137376954

training, and so on, and in this way prepare people of African descent for full public life.

One of the church-inspired organizations that gathered African Americans from a variety of locations for work related to political reform based on moral advancement was the "Negro Convention Movement" (1830–1864). It drew commitment from independent black Methodist churches, black Baptist churches as well as Presbyterian and Congregationalist African Americans. By means of this movement there developed an ecumenical push for political freedom for enslaved African Americans premised on a reading and practice of the Christian faith through a lens of allegiance to Christ as allegiance to the full freedom of all humanity.

This attention to moral reform also sparked involvement in boycotts of goods made by slave labor, and other public activities such as protest against the colonization scheme to send African Americans back to Africa as orchestrated by the American Colonization Society. Others, during the nineteenth century, would oppose the efforts of this Society based on its racist implications. Figures like Alexander Crummell opposed the forced movement of African Americans to Africa as a means to secure the United States for white Americans, and they opposed colonization of Africa by Europeans. What they favored, in sum, was the emigration of African Americans to Africa as part of a religious-socio-political obligation in line with the demands of the faith. This push back to Africa would allow African Americans to fulfill God's will for the advancement of people of African descent. Such forms of early African American religious nationalism, buttressed in part through missionary efforts, re-focused the goal of progress and moral reform away from the United States and placed it squarely on the revival and reclaiming of Africa.

The Civil War and Reconstruction would mark for many African American Christians the culmination of their efforts, and the initiation of a golden age. Yet, within a short period of time, they would find themselves addressing the nadir of African American public life as new forms of discrimination and systems of violence subdued political will for African American involvement in the socio-economic, political, and cultural workings of the Nation's public existence and public discourse. Yet, even such changes didn't deaden the assumption on the part of thinkers such as W. E. B. Du Bois that the fate of the United States was tied to its treatment of African Americans. There was something

DOI: 10.1057/9781137376954

messianic about this perception that continued at least in the shadows of African American church thought.

Notes

1   "Isaac H. Hunter to Brooklyn Start," in John W. Blassingame, editor. *Slave Testimony: Two Centuries of Letters, Speeches, Interviews, and Autobiographies* (Baton Rouge: Louisiana State University Press, 1977), 47–48.

2   Quoted in Albert Raboteau, *Slave Religion: The "Invisible Institution" in the Antebellum South* (New York: Oxford University Press, 1978), 268.

3   Raboteau, *Slave Religion*, 131.

4   C. Eric Lincoln and Lawrence H. Mamiya, *The Black Church in the African American Experience* (Durham: Duke University Press, 1990), 26.

5   Wilson Jeremiah Moses, "The Black Jeremiad and American Messianic Traditions," in Moses, *Black Messiahs and Uncle Toms: Social and Literary Manipulations of a Religious Myth* (University Park: The Pennsylvania State University Press, 1982), 31–38.

6   Quoted in Carol V. R. George, *Segregated Sabbaths: Richard Allen and the Rise of Independent Black Churches, 1760–1840* (New York: Oxford University Press, 1973), 126.

7   George, *Segregated Sabbaths*, 127.

8   Peter Paris, *The Social Teaching of the Black Churches* (Philadelphia: Fortress Press, 1985), 61.

DOI: 10.1057/9781137376954

2
Growing a Religious Agenda for Public Life

Abstract: *This chapter explores the growth of black churches after the Civil War, and the effort of these churches to use available resources to address the spiritual and political needs of African Americans. Such work, often framed in terms of the Social Gospel, involved the development of educational outlets and community organizations meant to address a range of concerns and needs. It also gives attention to social reform activities as well as efforts of African American clergy to enter US politics. Churches, in this chapter, point to the larger context of competing faith claims also interested in spiritual and material well-being.*

Pinn, Anthony B. *What Has the Black Church to Do with Public Life?* New York: Palgrave Macmillan, 2013.
DOI: 10.1057/9781137376954.

DOI: 10.1057/9781137376954

Some independent African American churches claimed hundreds of members. Yet, it is not until the increased mobility of traveling ministers made possible by the Civil War and Reconstruction, along with ability of former enslaved Africans to dictate their own lives, that self-sustaining black denominations experienced growth patterns in membership and organizational structure that defined their ability to impact private and public life. African American ministers from churches in the North moved South following the trail marked out by the Union army and encountered freed African Americans eager to express their new status through selection of a church home. Itinerate ministers played on this desire by emphasizing that joining an independent African American denomination was the best way to demonstrate independence of thought and practice.[1] Their argument worked.

Although the numbers can never be presented with full certainty, according to some accounts, there were almost 500,000 African Americans in churches in the South shortly before the Civil War. It is estimated, however, that by 1870 the number of African American Baptists alone would be nearly 500,000, with that number increasing into seven figures before the end of the first decade of the twentieth century.[2] Not only did the number of African American Methodists and Baptists grow, but the infrastructure to support this growth also advanced. For example, the number of African American Baptist ministers increased from almost 6,000 to roughly 17,000 in the 16-year period between 1890 and 1906. The African American Methodists also experienced rapid growth. The African Methodist Episcopal Church drew from roughly 20,000 around the time of the Civil War to almost 500,000 before 1900. The African Methodist Episcopal Church Zion had a membership of roughly 350,000 before 1900, and, lagging a bit behind, the Colored (later Christian) Methodist Episcopal Church had a membership of a little over 100,000 by 1890.[3] "Within forty years after emancipation, however, a black population of 8.3 million contained 2.7 million church members." Some scholars even claim a total membership closer to 4 million by 1906.[4]

Altered approaches to public activity in a time of "freedom"

Publishing interests and outlets (both Baptist and Methodist) as well as highly organized missionary efforts also provided a means by

DOI: 10.1057/9781137376954

which to advance thought regarding socio-political and economic arrangements.

If nothing else, the development and maintenance of denominational structures and leadership hierarchies provided participation in politics on a religious-micro level as "practice" for political involvement on the macro or national level. In addition, this "practice" also involved opportunities to work through cultural, social, and economic issues (tied to race and, at times, gender) within the relative safety—i.e., African American owned and operated—of the Black church world.

The religious world and the political world were intertwined, although not engaged evenly by African Americans.

Whether concerned with the politics of individual salvation, the politics of racial advancement, or some combination of the two—the bulk of those within black churches did not think transformation of any type—spiritual or physical—within the structures of life in the United States would happen without their input.

As historian Paul Harvey aptly notes, the new framing of freedom was multi-directional and multi-layered, involving the physical arrangements of African American life, the psychological and emotional redefining of personhood and humanity, and the affirmation of rightness of spiritual assumptions drawn from the religious heritage of African Americans. Political liberation's moral dimension was often named through the rhetoric of redemption, at other times simply the will of God. One might expect this grammar of existential change when one considers the theological tendency to think of the carnage of the Civil War as a divine test or punishment for the moral and ethical failings of the United States. The mere scope of suffering and pain, the tragic loss of life on both sides of the war had to point to more than political failure in a generic sense. From the perspective of black church members, it pointed to a deeper moral failure.[5] What was clear for many ministers and congregants was the manner in which the new narrative of the United States as a land marked by legal freedom was the requirement for blending religious insights and political commitments.

Churches developed community organizations providing educational opportunities related to issues of moral conduct and ethics for the urban context. Much of this revolved around techniques to avoid the harsher ramifications of discrimination. Some churches were involved in politics through support for labor activities and campaigns for just employment opportunities, and this extended to distribution of information

DOI: 10.1057/9781137376954

concerning politics and political figures in local areas. These efforts typically replaced attempts to secure and maintain political positions like those held briefly by African American ministers on the national, state, and local level during Reconstruction. For instance, Henry McNeal Turner of the African Methodist Episcopal Church was elected to state office in Georgia (1868), but racial hostility prevented him from actually occupying that office. Baptist minister Hiram Revels (Mississippi) became the first African American elected to Congress (1870), and African Methodist Episcopal Church minister Richard Cain serviced on both the state level (1873–1875) and nationally as a member of the House of Representatives (1877–1879).

Limited involvement in actual political processes and decision-making by such ministers elected to office was the general story. Yet, according to some nineteenth century church leaders, the political activism of African Americans during Reconstruction rested almost solely on the efforts of churches. They, writes Montgomery, "served as venues for political rallies and Republican Party meetings, and many ministers preached the message of the party about as often as the gospel of spiritual salvation." In this regard, black churches considered themselves the best means by which to inject race sensitive morality into the discussion of democratic life. Black churches offered political conversation laced by optimism made possible through the safeguards of their theologized faith—piety and politics.⁶

While Methodists and Baptists dominated the religious landscape of African American communities during the eighteenth and nineteenth centuries, the beginning of the twentieth century—marked by Jim Crow racial restrictions and customs—also framed a new spiritual energy concerned with sanctification and holiness. A Pentecostal experience drawn from the biblical book of the Acts of the Apostles, by means of which Christians could leave a life marked by spiritual perfection, gave rise to important developments such as the Church of God in Christ which is now the largest African American Pentecostal denomination in the country. Despite what some have argued, this concern with a Pentecostal experience marked by energetic worship and sanctification did not rule out involvement in public issues of a political nature. To the contrary, some scholars argue this concern with inner spiritual well-being was connected to a critique of racial discrimination, in that right relationship with God demanded proper conduct in one's mundane life.⁷

DOI: 10.1057/9781137376954

"What would Jesus do?"

This phrase, popular during the 1990s, is shadowed by a similar sentiment felt almost a century ago by advocates of Pentecostalism. But it takes on a particular significance, both spiritual and secular, for Pentecostals through a synergistic relationship between the signs of spiritual renewal (e.g., strong morals, ethics, and spiritual gifts such as "speaking in tongues") and the physical manifestations of this spiritual strength (e.g., demands for equality, recognition of the humanity of African Americans, and public safety against racist attack). For example, Pentecostalism takes root—through services in Los Angeles led by William Seymour—in a context of racial togetherness and without typical markers of racial discrimination. Even in this subtle rejection of Jim Crow, one finds a push for church involvement in the critique and correction of society's misdeeds in light of moral authority and spiritual power brought to bear on the workings of the secular world.

Much of this energy regarding the public presence and impact of black churches after the Civil War grows out of the needs of African Americans involved in the "Great Migration"—the large-scale movement of some 7 million African Americans out of the rural south and into cities in the North and South, as well as a movement to the West—taking place from the period of the Civil War through the mid-twentieth century. It was understood by many as an Exodus consistent theologically with the biblical account of the movement of the Children of Israel. In both instances, the objective was spiritual and material to the extent it involved the movement of God's people for new life opportunities in more accommodating environments. By means of the system of railroads, African Americans traversed geography hoping for greater life meaning and relief from the more challenging dimensions of life in a country marked by both promise and discrimination.[8] As part of this shift, northern and southern dimensions of African American Christian life were blended, resulting in a somewhat novel period of church growth and religious-theological re-evaluation.[9]

The shifts in the cartography of African American communities are noteworthy. In New York, the African American population grew by more than 50% in just the decade between 1900 and 1910. The African American population of Atlanta increased by over 40% during the same decade, and Chicago's African American presence grew by some 30%

DOI: 10.1057/9781137376954

within that same time period.[10] Evidence suggests those migrants who had religious commitments prior to moving maintained their religious faith and commitments in their new locations.

Rural churches in the south lost membership as a consequence of this movement, but urban churches grew, and when social and cultural differences prevented migrants from "fitting" into mainstream, African American churches in the cities, these migrants developed new churches.

Established urban churches found it difficult to absorb such large numbers, and the leadership of these churches argued they did not have the resources necessary to meet the needs of the African American migrants.

Providing opportunities for worship wouldn't begin to address the needs of African Americans during the Great Migration. Some churches worked to incorporate new arrivals and established programs to address their educational, socio-economic, recreational, and political needs. Activism required a keen balance between spiritual growth in the form of worship, Bible study, and other markers of soul-searching within the context of church activities, and attention to the application of church resources to public life.

Migration, of course, did not mean an end to worries nor did it short-circuit the most brutal forms of injustice. Lynching and other forms of violence and post-Reconstruction mechanisms of terror made it difficult for African Americans to see the practical and political value of their religious sensibilities at all times. Such terror called into question the ability of these sensibilities to circumvent all modes of racial animosity and oppression. Appearing more and more suspect, religious sensibilities seemed at best fragile—good intentioned, but not always a productive outlet for public engagement.

Churches sought to buttress the best values and morals of the faith over against what they perceived as the moral slippage in world conflict. Some of this sentiment is reflected in the goals of the National Afro-American Council (1899), a part of which was composed of church leaders:

1   To investigate and make an impartial report of all lynchings and other outrages perpetrated upon American citizens.
2   To assist in testing the constitutionality of laws which are made for the express purpose of oppressing the Afro-American.

DOI: 10.1057/9781137376954

3 To promote the work of securing legislation which in the individual state shall secure to all citizens the rights guaranteed them by the Thirteenth, Fourteenth, and Fifteenth Amendments to the Constitution of the United States.

4 To work in the aid of prison reform.

5 To recommend a healthy migration from terror-ridden sections of our land to states where law is respected and maintained.

6 To encourage both industrial and higher education.

7 To promote business enterprises among the people.

8 To educate sentiment on all lines that specially affect [sic] our race.

9 To inaugurate and promote plans for the moral elevation of the Afro-American people.

10 To urge the appropriation for a school fund by the federal government to provide education for citizens who are denied school privileges by discriminating state Laws.[11]

Notions of "freedom," "equality," "citizenship," and "personhood" remained important components of the lexicon of black life as expressed within the context of churches. But, expression of these principles in the daily existence of African Americans became difficult for churches and church leaders to predict: their code of morality and ethics with respect to public life took a blow—not fatal, but substantial. At times, even the most radical political activism seemed to pale in comparison to the socio-cultural assault on African Americans that portrayed African Americans as inherently inferior and a danger to civil society—a danger that should be met with great force. These efforts to dehumanize African Americans fueled popular imagination in ways that reinforced political effort to maintain clear distinctions between whites and blacks.

Two world wars and the glaring disregard for African Americans (even during these periods of national crisis) only re-enforced the socio-political marginality of African Americans. Churches encouraged the participation of African Americans in these challenges to the United States as a way of securing the appreciation of the Nation in gratitude for the sacrifice on behalf of a country that had not treated them properly. The outcome, however, was not what churches and other African American organizations intended. African Americans fought and died for the Nation, but the general structures of racial injustice remained intact.

DOI: 10.1057/9781137376954

The Social Gospel and the secular

Clearly, this is not to suggest that the moral anchoring of African American communities was lost with this blow; rather, it is to note the manner in which other organizations—fraternal organizations, schools, social societies, and so on provide alternate sources of moral outlook and ethical parameters for proper living.

Churches continued to play a role but their monopoly on visions of morality and ethics with respect to public life was brought into fundamental question through the emergence of a rich and complex structuring of collective life in African American communities, in urban areas both north and south. The form of this involvement entailed variations on the theme of the "Social Gospel"—the idea that Christian faith should have felt consequences in the various realms of physical life.

Women, who typically had fewer opportunities for formal leadership within black churches (e.g., pastorates), did some of the more radical work related to the participation of religious communities in public issues. Figures such as Mary McLeod Bethune—a Methodist—made great strides in securing educational opportunities for African Americans as a religiously based (as the Christian orientation of the University bearing her name would attest) mechanism for advancing African Americans through knowledge. Christian community leader Ida B. Wells combined the ethics of faith with a keen sense of the socio-political and cultural framings for injustice in ways meant to impact both the activism of African Americans and legal protections in accordance with the Constitution.

In addition, Wells' work informed and her contacts enhanced the efforts of African Methodist Episcopal (AME) minister Reverdy C. Ransom, who sought to bring the moral and ethical sensibilities of the Christian story to bear on the socio-political and economic issues of the twentieth century—labor, social opportunities, and political progressive strategies. The idea under-girding this social Christianity involved an assumption that Christian values when brought to contemporary issues provided strategies for improving the public arena. And Baptist layperson Nannie H. Burroughs gathered resources and workers to aid migrants who made their way to the North.

It is important to recognize that many black churches remained numerically small and without the populations and resources necessary

DOI: 10.1057/9781137376954

to play a significant role in the public affairs of their particular locales. But as far as figures like Wells, Ransom, and Burroughs were concerned, individual spiritual health combined with political sensitivities promoted a place for churches in public life.

Some churches extended their efforts beyond church-housed programming to include efforts cutting across local arrangements. For two more recent examples, the two largest African American Baptist denominations—the National Baptist Convention, USA and the National Baptist Convention of America—formed the Minority Enterprise Financial Acquisition Corporation to provide financial assistance with the development of housing. Familiar to many is Operation PUSH (People United to Save Humanity)—the Rainbow PUSH Action Network as of 1996—an organization developed by Rev. Jesse Jackson to foster socio-political and economic progress mindful of the moral and ethical commitments that frame the country's vision for collective life. Whether in the form of group effort or the programming of individual churches, much of the work done in the public arena has involved education, housing, business development, and training. As C. Eric Lincoln and Lawrence Mamiya note, "politics in black churches involves more than the exercise of power on behalf of a constituency; it also includes the community building and empowering activities in which many black churches, clergy, and lay members participate in daily."[12]

Whether through direct involvement of ministers in politics or through attention given to them by politicians seeking votes, churches became a lynchpin of political conversation and energy. A push for political involvement, for shaping public policy with respect to race, marked the radicalization of the Black church, which scholars such as Gayraud Wilmore discuss as the highpoint of the Black church's public profile. However, many black churches spiritualized their mission and avoided public activism. They argued for a primary role in the spiritual renewal of African Americans, with secular organizations such as the National Association for the Advancement of Colored People (NAACP) and the National Urban League (NUL) taking care of other concerns. Wilmore labels this position the deradicalization of the Black church and the de-spiritualization of social protest.[13]

Churches maintained activity with regard to African American life, but for some this was achieved through a prioritizing of the spiritual. These churches understood the development of the soul as the primary means by which to develop the best moral compass, and in turn that

DOI: 10.1057/9781137376954

moral compass would guide all areas of life. A stereotype of this thinking involves an assumption that such churches have no interest in external activities—that they are passive and silent in the public arena. According to some, it is more accurate to see this spiritual emphasis as a privileging of a certain type of public involvement and profile as opposed to absence of this dimension of "church work". More politically involved churches appreciated the spiritual needs of humans, but also recognized the function of churches related to the physical needs of African Americans. This did not involve a spirit-out approach but rather a synergy between spiritual growth and socio-political and economic health by means of which each fed the other.

In some cases, from the late twentieth century through the first decade of the twenty-first century, the mega-church phenomenon has provided a caricature of that perspective through a preoccupation with prosperity as the mark of spiritual health. However, this sense of prosperity is typically without social critique of the sources of poverty and injustice. Churches holding to this spiritualized perspective, although most certainly did not, maintained the need for church-sponsored support for African Americans such as food pantries, schools, business training, etc., but they also recognized these localized programs must be combined with changes in governmental policies and practices that address the larger dynamics of race-based discrimination. To act otherwise was to deny the ministry of Christ and the essence of Christ-like morality and ethics.

Scholars and those who read academic treaties on black churches typically present this tension through a typology of motivation: "this-worldly" and "other-worldly" frameworks of purpose. While the former is privileged in that it most easily represents the type of progressive engagement with key issues that appeal to liberal sensibilities, the latter finds few supporters within academic circles. And, those who do attempt to justify this posture toward activity in the world tend to position it as a more spiritually centered form of progressive activism (to the extent it can be viewed as a critique of racism at both the existential and ontological levels of discourse and human meaning).

Other options?

Whether critiquing or embracing black churches in ways sensitive to Wilmore's theory, it is important to keep in mind the non-church based

DOI: 10.1057/9781137376954

modalities of activism serving as competition for black churches in public life.

In the 1920s, for instance, some African Americans turned to the radical politics of the Communist Party, assuming this move would allow for more sustained attention to race as a political issue. They rejected the church on grounds that it was apolitical and committed to a theology of subservience.

The activities of Marcus Garvey during the same period of time also drew some of the energy away from black churches by providing alternate outlets for political energy that revolved around a grand connection to Africa and limited attention to the traditional theological vocabulary and structures that dominated the nineteenth century.

During this period, the religious landscape also came to include traditions blending doctrines and ritual structures from a variety of traditions. For example, Father Divine's Peace Mission altered Christian theism by naming him God, and Sweet Daddy Grace's House of Prayer for All Peoples combined elements of Pentecostalism with dimensions of New Thought. Furthermore, black spiritual churches combined elements of Pentecostalism, Roman Catholicism, and African-based traditional practices associated with Voodoo. All of these new traditions, however, maintained some commitment to the public life of adherents through approaches to greater economic success and through a re-thinking of social relationships. This is particularly the case with Father Divine, whose Peace Mission had black and white members and no social distinction was made based on race. Father Divine also provided economic resources to those in need during the Great Depression—when many organizations religious and secular were losing ground.

The Nation of Islam develops during this period (1930), and while the number of members is uncertain, its impact on perceptions of African Americans and African American religion is noteworthy. Playing on doctrinal elements of Islam and Christianity, the Nation of Islam maintained a conservative economic and political agenda, but a radical theology that posited Master Fard Muhammad as God incarnate—with African Americans representing the people created by God (Allah) for greatness and glory, and whites being made by a mad scientist for the purpose of destruction.

The more charged elements of its theology would grow to have only metaphorical significance (e.g., white supremacy is demonic, not white

DOI: 10.1057/9781137376954

Americans) as the organization transitioned from the leadership of Elijah Muhammad, to Warith Deen Muhammad, and then Louis Farrakhan. Noteworthy is the fact that under the leadership of Farrakhan members of the Nation of Islam were encouraged to vote and hold political office. Always vocal in terms of social transformation, this foray into politics begins in earnest when Farrakhan supported publicly the presidential candidacy of Reverend Jesse Jackson—and it grows to include members of the movement involved in local politics.

Black churches could no longer argue that they were the only organizations with the capacity for large-scale attention to socio-political issues effecting African Americans. Nonetheless, "despite the emergence of secular agencies such as the Urban League and the cooperation of such groups as the Travelers' Aid Society," writes historian Milton Sernett, "African American churches remained at the center of the northern institutional response" to the challenges of the Great Migration and the dynamics of racialized northern life.[14]

The Great Migration that continued well into the twentieth century would help to refine political involvement as churches in urban areas gained socio-political standing with white politicians through their ability to deliver blocs of votes but also to move once again—also through these voting blocs—into political arenas. Chicago provides an example of this, as Oscar De Priest gained political office in local politics before becoming a member of Congress—the first African American elected to Congress in the twentieth century. Using churches to both discuss politics and organizing votes continued into the mid-twentieth century. As Mary Fair Burks, a Baptist who founded the Women's Political Council during the Montgomery Bus Boycott (1955–1956) remarked,

> As chairman of the Political Action Committee of the Dexter Avenue Baptist church—a committee formed by Dr. King—following church services, I would read the names of the candidates whom we had decided were the least objectionable...Other churches initiated similar practices.[15]

Notes

1   William E. Montgomery, *Under Their Own Vine and Fig Tree: The African-American Church in the South, 1865–1900* (Baton Rouge: Louisiana State University), 97–98.

DOI: 10.1057/9781137376954

2   C. Eric Lincoln and Lawrence H. Mamiya, *The Black Church in the African American Experience* (Durham: Duke University Press, 1990), 25; Paul Harvey, *Freedom's Coming: Religious Culture and the Shaping of the South from the Civil War through the Civil Rights Era* (Chapel Hill: University of North Carolina, 2008), 8.

3   Lincoln and Mamiya, *Black Church in the African American Experience*, 25, 54, 58, 63.

4   Albert Raboteau, *Slave Religion: The "Invisible Institution" in the Antebellum South* (New York: Oxford University Press, 1978), 209; Harvey, *Freedom's Coming*, 8.

5   Harvey, *Freedom's Coming*, 6–7.

6   Montgomery, *Under Their Own Vine and Fig Tree*, 163.

7   See, for instance, Cheryl Sanders, *Saints in Exile: The Holiness-Pentecostal Experience in African American Religion and Culture* (New York: Oxford University Press, 1999).

8   John M. Giggie, *After Redemption: Jim Crow and the Transformation of African American Religion in the Delta, 1875–1915* (New York: Oxford University Press, 2008), chapter 1.

9   Milton C. Sernett, *Bound for the Promised Land: African American Religion and the Great Migration* (Durham: Duke University Press, 1997), 4.

10 Gayraud S. Wilmore, *Black Religion and Black Radicalism: An Interpretation of the Religious History of African Americans*, 3rd Edition (Maryknoll, NY: Orbis Books, 1998), 171.

11 Reverdy C. Ransom, "A Program for the Negro," in Anthony B. Pinn, editor. *Making the Gospel Plain: The Writings of Bishop Reverdy C. Ransom* (Harrisburg: Trinity Press International, 1999), 195.

12 Lincoln and Mamiya, *Black Church in the African American Experience*, 199.

13 Wilmore, *Black Religion and Black Radicalism*, chapters 6–7.

14 Sernett, *Bound for the Promised Land*, 138.

15 Quoted in Anthony B. Pinn, *The Black Church in the Post-Civil Rights Era* (Maryknoll, NY: Orbis Books, 2002), 14.

DOI: 10.1057/9781137376954

3

The "Golden Age" of Black Churches in Public

Abstract: *Continuing attention to changes in the religious landscape of African American communities fostered by the Great Migration, this chapter explores the confrontation between religion and public life framed by the civil rights movement and post-civil rights activities related to issues such as HIV/AIDS. The public work of black churches is placed in relationship to the social critique and activism of figures such as Malcolm X. Attention is given to the development of radical theologies such as black theology and womanist theology that emerge during the late twentieth century.*

Pinn, Anthony B. *What Has the Black Church to Do with Public Life?* New York: Palgrave Macmillan, 2013.
DOI: 10.1057/9781137376954.

The period between the Civil War and the civil rights movement marked growing class stratification within African American communities—highlighted by the growth of a middle class including ministers, morticians, small business owners, and so on. This class stratification, made more intense and visible through urbanization, resulted in a growing debate concerning the needs of African Americans and the best strategies for securing the resources to meet these needs. According to sociologist C. Eric Lincoln,

> with the concentration of large numbers of black people in the cities came a greater awareness of African Americans as a distinct social group. Through the labor movement, urban black workers were exposed to the protest tactics and possibilities of organizing for social change. Black churches grew in size, establishing relationships with one another through citywide and later statewide ministerial alliances. In addition to this vital communication network, new modes of communication—radio, telephones, movies and later television—presented themselves.[1]

That is to say, the political inclinations of black churches were expressed with respect to electoral politics but also in terms of "community building and empowering activities" that gained limited media attention and public notice.[2] In short, the political activities of black churches seek at least implicitly to appeal to the "in the world (but not of it)" dimension of their theological-ideological posture toward the mundane aspects of life.

While some academics—such as sociologist E. Franklin Frazier—raised questions concerning the nature and function of black churches as well as the collective merit of their work, popular opinion involved attention to these organizations as vital to the safety and advancement of African Americans.

This is not to say there weren't calls for churches to better recognize and address their public obligations. However, overall there seemed a sense that African American communities were better because of the work done by these churches, or at the very least these churches had the potential for great and positive impact. In fact, due to the effects of racial discrimination, some African Americans relied on the assistance of churches so as to avoid physical confrontation with substandard care from organizations in the larger society.

DOI: 10.1057/9781137376954

Black churches front and center?

By the mid-twentieth century assumptions concerning the public capacities of black churches would be put to the test through the demands and struggles of the civil rights movement.

While social Christianity of the early twentieth century provided a theological stepping-stone for non-violent direct action against racial injustice, a more aggressive push into the public arena by black churches also brought into quick relief tensions regarding the best approach to issues of socio-political progress. That the epicenter of this tension between certain church values and political agitation would be in the South should come as no surprise in that, despite the Great Migration, the majority of African Americans lived in the South and the modes of racial discrimination were there most graphic.

A triadic structure of need and resource made the South ground zero for civil rights activism during the mid-twentieth century—and to some extent grew out of an old sense of domestic missions, "benevolent work," and the Social Gospel emphasis on a practical faith. There was also something in this of a lingering perception that proper and moral behavior would win the day and cause reluctant white Americans to move in the direction of racial equality and socio-political and economic justice. This was the optimism, the idealism, fostered through the religious posture of those in the churches—and it was maintained, largely, even in the face of counter arguments and evidence (e.g., legal segregation and restrictions).[3] Churches believed at least implicitly that instilling in African Americans social skills and proper attitudes toward morally balanced individual and collective life would position them to participate in every dimension of US democratic processes. Civil rights activities assumed the correctness of this thinking and simply expanded the arenas in which this could be practiced—boycotts, sit-ins, marches, and so on.

Albeit not the first nor the only church leader whose participation gave some moral-ethical shape and theological framing for mid-twentieth century protest, Martin Luther King, Jr., is commonly referenced as the most prominent leader—the one whose perception of the United States and its potential offered the logic of struggle and legitimized the sacrifices made by advocates of social transformation. As scholars of Martin L. King, Jr. have argued for decades now, King—and by extension

DOI: 10.1057/9781137376954

the Christian wing of the civil rights movement—drew on morality and socio-political interests that marked the Black church Tradition from its initial development through the twentieth century. He put into play the Social Gospel perspective that shaped many black churches—and used its moral and ethical sensibilities as the proper lens through which to read and assess the practices of democracy in the United States. However, assumptions that black churches were well represented in the movement are unfounded.

Even King acknowledged the lack of participation of black churches. In fact, the Progressive National Baptist Convention developed in the early 1960s precisely because the National Baptist Convention, USA—the numerically largest black denomination—rejected the appeal by King for his father, Martin L. King, Sr., Reverend Gardner Taylor, and other ministers from the NBC, USA to play an active role in the civil rights strategies of direct action. According to King and others like him, non-violent direction action, the willingness to absorb violent attack, gave the protesters the moral high ground. The end result, the rationale continued, would be a society in which all participated equally as full citizens with all the accompanying rights and responsibilities.

Perhaps what best captured the synergy between the morality of black churches and their ethical commitments brought to bear on the dynamics of public and private life is found in the concept of the "Beloved Community" popularized by Martin L. King, Jr. By this concept, King meant to mark out cooperation, mutuality, and shared socio-political and economic opportunity based on the "Golden Rule."[4] As part of the discussion of the "Beloved Community", advocates of this framing of collective life urged personal conduct consistent with the teachings of the Christian faith and political conduct that recognized the humanity of every citizen.

The organizational structure for work toward this "Beloved Community" was the Southern Christian Leadership Conference (SCLC) made up of ministers from across various denominations. Composed of national leadership as well as local affiliates, the SCLC provided the vision and orchestrated the various activities associated with civil rights protests. The Christian emphasis and biblically based moral and ethical guidelines—combined with influences such as Gandhi—also took root in the student organization named Student Nonviolent Coordinating Committee (SNCC). With time, however, some members of SNCC were disillusioned with the tactics championed by King. Growing tired

DOI: 10.1057/9781137376954

of beatings and limited gains, members of the Student Nonviolent Coordinating Committee and others, once in line with King's philosophy of protest, began to argue for a more aggressive approach—one that recognized the potential of counter violence to achieve the desired political transformations.

The moral upper hand was of limited consequence for those of this opinion in that pointing out right and wrong was not the issue. Those perpetuating racial violence knew the codes, but the benefits of their practices outpaced any sense of moral obligation. The situation would change only when an equal force met the force of discrimination.

Malcolm X became the symbol of this perspective, particularly in northern communities where the techniques of discrimination differed from those in southern states. As national spokesperson for the Nation of Islam, Malcolm X ridiculed the efforts of King, SCLC, and the nonviolent civil rights movement. For Malcolm X, at least with respect to his rhetoric, violence was a viable option. To think African Americans could muster the resources to meet violence with violence was fantasy according to King, and it was inconsistent with the Christian gospel. Malcolm X, on the other hand, held to a social theory of public life in the United States that assumed white Americans would never willingly surrender power, and a country founded in violence would not respect a people unwilling to fight back. This is all ironic in that the Nation of Islam never initiated explicit political violence nor did members of the organization defend themselves against attack.

Some of Malcolm X's socio-political opinions would change after he left the Nation of Islam; yet, his assassination in 1965 prevented the full development of his new mosque and the realization of his desire to participate in the civil rights movement through a new organization called the Organization for Afro-American Unity. Nonetheless, he captured an audience and marked the alternative to King's approach.

Theology and power

Some African American Christians saw no need to pick between the social critique of Malcolm X and the Social Gospel advocated by Martin L. King, Jr.

Instead, a synthesis was proposed and named black theology of liberation. What this move offered was a more radical sense of the Social

DOI: 10.1057/9781137376954

Gospel, one in which Jesus the Christ was understood as having been a black revolutionary concerned with the liberation of the oppressed. In this sense, God privileges the oppressed and works for their advancement by all means.

Marked by this theological and ethical shift was a re-thinking of the Black church. One of the early and graphic examples involved the *New York Times* piece by the National Conference of Black Churchmen (1966) in which a "black theology" was announced as the revitalized thinking of progressive black churches. This collective of clergy and professional academics pooled their intellectual resources and shared passion for an activist faith to respond to shortcomings: Martin L. King, Jr., did not recognize the true nature of racism and the full and revolutionary potential of the Christian faith; and the black power movement failed to recognize the liberative potential of the Christian faith.

Led by theologian James Cone and others, this group's black theology argued that God is on the side of the oppressed (in this case, African Americans suffering from racism and its consequences), and the Bible speaks to this through the story of the Exodus and the Christ Event. In both instances, God provides deliverance for suffering people.

Newspaper pieces and public talks were followed by formal academic texts further outlining this approach to theology and ethics. Rather than simple moral adjustments as suggested by earlier church leaders and mainline civil rights leaders that assumed the conduct of African Americans would encourage new attention to full citizenship, black theology exercised a bit more pessimism regarding the motivation of white Americans. And, in light of this new social theory and politicized theological anthropology, force might be necessary to secure the socio-economic and political equality required by African Americans.

The demand for "Black Power" could inform Christianity-based praxis. Yet, not lost here was concern with "moral suasion" through massaging of "moral guilt" as founder of black theology James Cone noted as far back as 1984.[5] In this way, black theological language is more aggressive and its anger much more apparent and visceral, but the general posture toward the needs of African Americans continued to hinge on socio-political and economic change that privileged the power of moral arguments. However, unlike many earlier figures, black theologians attempted to offer a nuanced critique of black churches for failing to put the material welfare of African Americans ahead of their own self-interest (i.e., desire for continued mainstream

DOI: 10.1057/9781137376954

status and the favor of those in power). Yet, a growing desire for deep connections to the Black church on the part of early black theologians circumvented sustained attention to any shortcomings on the part of black churches.

What became evident to many within the first decade of black theology's existence were the other forms of oppression not covered by the activism of black churches and the rhetoric of black theologians.

At their best, black churches had developed a way of thinking and community-centered activities that challenged the race-based socio-economic and political shortcomings of the country. Yet, they did little to address the gender discrimination in black churches and the larger society. Women had limited opportunities to exercise leadership in churches beyond those functions that were consistent with the "cult of domesticity." In the secular work place, women fared no better. Black women within the Academy and some within churches fought against this injustice and critiqued gender discrimination. They called churches to accountability by exposing the way in which they mirrored the discriminatory attitudes they sought to end with regard to racism. This new theology was named "womanist theology" because it drew from the definition of womanish behavior offered by Alice Walker in 1982.[6]

The issue of gender uncovered in womanist scholarship was often connected to issues of sexuality, and this pushed churches into public thought and activity involving sexism, sexual violence, and health issues such as HIV/AIDS.

Regarding such issues, churches have played a public role in two ways—promoting a liberal agenda and others by advancing a conservative stance related to HIV/AIDS. Drawing from readings of the Bible, many black churches push moral judgment on HIV/AIDS—whether the results of drug use or sexual contact (particularly homosexual contact)—perceived as a sin. Furthermore, through a problematic theological logic, many churches privilege the concept of sin, and believe that sin comes with a price that must be paid by the sinner. For the most conservative black churches, this price can be pain and death. These same churches are those opposed to gay marriage and other models of relational living that run contrary to their particular reading of scripture and Church Tradition. Hence, this poses a problem: how should this be addressed in spiritual and physical terms? Would addressing the issue through programs and the pulpit come across as an endorsement of particular lifestyles and practices?

DOI: 10.1057/9781137376954

Ignoring the issue has resulted in the death of laypersons and clergy—without the means to creatively and successfully tackle the destructive nature of HIV/AIDS. Others address the issue, and do so in ways that avoid moral judgments but instead seek to value human life—through a commitment of the church to a public ministry with felt consequences for the physical needs of African Americans. A prime example of this is the Balm in Gilead's Black Church HIV/AIDS National Technical Assistance Center that provides educational resources, information, church-based programs of prayer, sermons related to the topic, and more.[7] The organization's efforts are meant to increase awareness and offer ways for churches to exercise their spiritual and secular capital for advances in HIV/AIDS as a health and health care issue as opposed to a moral and ethical concern. On the local level, some churches may not address the larger issues of policy related to HIV/AIDS but instead provide ministry related to taking care of the daily needs of those suffering with HIV/AIDS—such as meals, cleaning services, and visits to make certain the ill are not alone.

While a notable percentage of African American Christians traditionally have opposed more liberal stances on sexuality, some have understood the church's role to include non-judgmental ministry and assistance to those in need—recognizing the moral correctness of numerous lifestyles.

Organizations such as the Congress of National Black Churches worked to address healthcare, with a clear focus on illicit drug use through education programs meant to grow awareness and appropriate modes of engagement with victims. By the turn of the twenty-first century the Congress of National Black Churches, through thousands of clergy persons working in almost 40 cities, had contact with half a million people.[8]

Changing church demographics

It is worth noting that black and womanist theologies emerged and grew during a period of decline for black churches. Charges of anti-intellectualism in light of their general disinterest in the fine points of black theology, and the end of the major campaigns of the civil rights movement marked in a significant way by the killing of Martin Luther King, Jr., pointed to a decline in membership and activity.

DOI: 10.1057/9781137376954

The tension between community activism and individual piety seemed to shift in the direction of the latter. For some this was just another sign of the growing secularization of the United States, with the Black church simply being the next in a line of organizations to fall victim. This would involve an attempt on the part of some to limit the impact of religion to the private and to preserve the public arena for a less spiritually charged grammar of engagement.

In light of these arrangements, the question both implied and spoken in some quarters involved the real role of the Black church.

Did it represent privatized appeals to spiritual matters? Or, did it offer an organizational structure for advancing a political agenda? Better yet, was it some combination of the two? Had the Black church really played a significant role through forms of an ethic of love in the advancement of African Americans, or had it received credit for more than its thought and action actually brought about? Was it the Civil Rights Acts of 1964 and 1968, and the Equal Employment Opportunity Commission, that were responsible for the economic gains of African Americans?

Such questions framed a general lament of the Black church's declining significance, power, and moral authority. For some seeking a more radical and aggressive approach to socio-political and economic equality, the Black church had little to offer. For them, its connection to the Christian Tradition used to justify and shepherd racial inequality prevented it from functioning with a clear commitment to racial justice. In addition to this critique of black churches, a small but vocal black middle class explored non-church based ways for achieving socio-political and economic advancement.

Nonetheless, black churches have weathered these ideological storms. And while on some level damaged, they continue to hold a place in the imagination of whites and blacks alike.

There are still assumptions made—by both progressives and conservatives—regarding a public role for black churches. By the time of C. Eric Lincoln and Lawrence Mamiya's published study of black churches (1990), the average black church had a membership between 200 and 599, and had an annual income (for the majority of urban churches surveyed) of more than $50,000. A noteworthy percentage (40.8) of urban churches had some type of relationship to civil rights organizations, suggesting that these churches have a sense of public ministry involving the socio-political challenges facing African Americans. And of much interest, most churches during the period of the survey did

DOI: 10.1057/9781137376954

not participate in government-funded programs. Nonetheless, a majority of the ministers believed black and white churches have a different role to play in light of the manner in which issues of racism impact African Americans differently—resulting in the need for black churches to recognize injustice in a way white churches need not.[9]

Still, the question remains: should these churches have that type of public role? Or, as Manning Marable asks:

> Why has the Black Church as an institution failed repeatedly to evolve into a coherent agency promoting the liberation of Afro-American people, and why has it succeeded to reveal itself as an essential factor in Black struggles at certain difficult historical periods? ... Why, in short, does the Black Church continue to perform its fundamentally ambiguous role in the Black experience?[10]

Notes

1   C. Eric Lincoln and Lawrence H. Mamiya, *The Black Church in the African American Experience* (Durham: Duke University Press, 1990), 165.

2   Ibid., 199.

3   Milton C. Sernett, *Bound for the Promised Land: African American Religion and the Great Migration* (Durham: Duke University Press, 1997), 88–91, 115.

4   This refers to the following strategy: "Do unto others as you would have them do unto you."

5   James H. Cone, *For My People: Black Theology and the Black Church* (Maryknoll, NY: Orbis Books, 1984), 88–92.

6   Alice Walker, *In Search of Our Mothers' Gardens* (San Diego, CA: Harcourt, 1983), xi–xii.

7   See: www.balmingilead.org/. The African American lectionary also seeks to provide resource for addressing these issues within the context of worship. See: www.theafricanamericanlectionary.org/

8   Quoted in Anthony B. Pinn, *The Black Church in the Post-Civil Rights Era* (Maryknoll, NY: Orbis Books, 2002), 97.

9   Lincoln and Mamiya, *Black Church in the African American Experience*, 164–195.

10 Ibid., 227.

DOI: 10.1057/9781137376954

4

The Black Church's Public Profile—An Assessment

Abstract: *With the presentation of black churches within public life completed, this chapter assesses the impact of these activities. While, from the start, the presence of black churches within the public arena has been acknowledged, this chapter outlines the limitations and problems associated with this involvement. For example, the theological arrangements for these churches—including notions of cosmic authority—along with structural elements of their organizational frameworks hamper development of the proper posture toward public discourse.*

Pinn, Anthony B. *What Has the Black Church to Do with Public Life?* New York: Palgrave Macmillan, 2013.
DOI: 10.1057/9781137376954.

Even as members of the black middle class made their way back to churches in the 1990s, they did so for a variety of reasons—social networking, cultural connections—often having nothing to do with the theological-moral arguments made by pastors and formal church doctrine.

Their presence also raised questions concerning the role of the pastor in the church's internal and external efforts. Increasing educational opportunities and some advancement within professional life meant the pastor was not of necessity the most educated or most capable person in the church. Hence, leadership had to be shared, and had to be more communal and collective, and, this no doubt informed the Black church's public presence moving into the late 1990s. For example, according to Sidney Verba, "nearly 40 percent of African Americans practice organizing skills at their place of worship…"[1]

Furthermore, according to the 1999–2000 "Black Churches and Politics" survey, over 80% of those responding to the question indicated that their congregation had been involved in political activism such as voter registration. However, this survey found that of those indicating their congregations were very politically active during the civil right movement (25%), a much smaller percentage (15%) indicating that their churches were very active during the 1980s and 1990s.[2] It is also important to note that the Pew Charitable Trust found that African Americans surveyed are more likely to label themselves conservative (32%) or moderate (36%), with a smaller percentage claiming liberal (23%) as a marker of their ideological position; and, African Americans surveyed tend to affiliate with the Democratic Party.[3] This does not mean a lack of public involvement, but points out differing frames for understanding and analyzing problems faced.

As Wilmore and Lincoln note, the political dimension of black church public profile involves a matrix of survival forms, the preservation of a community based on the resources of a religious institution.[4] But proper participation in the public sphere must be premised on more than a survival impulse.

Such an impulse breeds types of exceptionalist philosophies and xenophobia that damage the great democratic potential lodged in the diversity of opinion within public-political debate. The moral authority that played so heavy a role in the public profile and activities of black churches was also brought into question through the indiscretions of some prominent African American ministers. A prime example is

Rev. Henry Lyons, whose career was derailed by charges of mismanaged financial resources belonging to the National Baptist Convention, USA, Inc., of which he was president. And this should be placed within the context of a generally low level of confidence in religious leaders in 1998 as reported by sociologist Mark Chaves.[5]

The church and morality as public

Moral judgment is a limited and limiting approach to the public arena. King's appeal to the conscience of the Nation left him frustrated and disillusioned, and continuing this approach produces little. Yet, moral judgment is instinctive for the Black church—lodged in the very nature and DNA of black church identity and purpose for over 200 years. In this way, over reliance on the Black church to alter the dynamics of life in African American communities is foolish.

Unlike Gary Marx, I am not suggesting that religion serves as an opiate that stifles involvement in public debate and activism.[6] Rather, I am suggesting certain forms of African American Christianity damage efforts to engage in the public life of African Americans. *Furthermore, churches by their very nature are not built for the type of work necessary to secure full participation in the democratic processes of life in the United States.* A book, the Bible, guides them. Far from democratic in nature, the Bible points in the direction of theocracy—human life premised on the will of unseen forces. And, the language for engagement offered by churches involves a theology of individualization, an ideology of human defect without the means for secular improvement in that fundamental corrections to human character can come only through God. *Black churches may serve as mechanisms of information transfer, gauging a sense of moral development on the level of the individual, but they are not equipped and positioned to determine the nature of that information.*

Furthermore, the communicative possibilities and impact of churches are affected by inadequate internal structures for delivery of services and information. These include ideological structures such as homophobia, theodicy renditions of moral evil, archaic notions of sexual purity, and others that do damage to segments of the African American population. Much of this is guided by strong attention to biblical stories and principles as unquestionably relevant to contemporary life. There are flaws to this approach: black churches have worked based on an assumption of

DOI: 10.1057/9781137376954

pathology—a failure to conform to rules and regulations of life exemplified or rendered normative.

An additional problem is the assumption that black churches are best equipped to do this public work because they are numerically significant and have a national infrastructure.

Recent studies indicate roughly 87% of African Americans claim affiliation with a religious institution and claim religion is important in their personal lives, and 76% of African Americans surveyed claim to pray daily and 88% of them claim a belief in God. In addition, a significant percentage of African Americans believe religion should play a role in the public sphere and should factor into the attitudes and actions of political leaders.[7] High levels of religiosity, however, do not mean it is safe to assume this personal religious commitment can translate into a mechanism for public discourse and resulting national policies.

Churches may help African American participants develop a sense of individual identity and group identification, but this sense of self and belonging isn't devoid of the schizophrenic tendencies of the Black church's teachings—insider/outsider dichotomies; epistemological openness and epistemological exclusiveness; xenophobia and missionary impulse; and so on.

Black churches have had a mixed relationship to the larger social system—at times supporting the normative claims and practices of society and at other points critiquing (while exercising inconsistent struggle against) the socio-political and economic strictures imposed against African Americans. This love-hate relationship with the "American Way of Life" results in organizational schizophrenia that prohibits the development of consistently clear rhetoric regarding, and actions related to, the plight of African Americans. And, it fixes public discourse within frameworks of "sin" as moral standing and this spiritualization of social defects does not posit socio-political and economic strategies capable of working outside a matrix of transhistorical regulation.

This is not to rule out morality. It is simply to say that morality framing activity and outcomes within the public arena should draw from a larger range of source materials than the Christian faith—and this framing of morality should not privilege a particular religious community's thinking and discourse.

The problem is not moral shortcoming or decency in perception of the good. It is larger than this and can't be addressed by churches in sustainable ways. They assume in/outside groups. Furthermore,

DOI: 10.1057/9781137376954

theological rationales fail to account for existential developments and concerns. And, political developments are not properly addressed through churches in that they are businesses, and also institutions with a spiritual foundation not bound by what is reasonable. They have a language and grammar too narrow for public exchange and discourse and offer no good way of thinking through the distribution of resources.

Religion may provide fortitude on the personal level and some degree of energy with a limited half-life in the public sphere, but it lacks the scope and capacity to serve as the organizing principle of public life for African Americans, or any Americans. And while a high percentage of African Americans claim particular elements of a Christian world-view such as belief in God, this is not matched by consistent church attendance.

The segment of the African American population least involved in the Black church, young black men, is also the portion of the African American population most at risk—with high rates of unemployment, low educational achievement levels, and disproportionate contact with the justice system. One argument might be that the lack of participation in churches accounts on some level for the unchecked plight of young African American males. However, one might also ask what are churches failing to provide that accounts for this lack of participation and what are their shortcomings with respect to the public discourse on socio-political and economic justice that leaves unchecked the targeting of African American males.

The Nation of Islam, for example, offered a response to this question that brought to task African Americans—particularly African American males. During the "Million Man March," Minister Louis Farrakhan led a rather large gathering of African American men through a process of repentance and reconstitution of individual and communal commitment. This led to a revived and rigorous moral code that mirrored the familial ideals and gender dynamics guiding public discourse, one that has guided so many African Americans for several centuries. In this way, the moral vision of the Nation of Islam and that of many black churches are in line—but offer very little that suggest this vision should serve as the basic framework for public discourse and policy.

Black churches have had limited involvement in issues of public policy, but instead have had a hand in servicing basic needs through meal programs, health care (such as testing for high blood pressure and diabetes)

DOI: 10.1057/9781137376954

education, and the like.[8] And I argue this limitation has occurred for good reason.

Churches, as historian Gayraud Wilmore has noted, interact in the public arena with an intention that is marked by survival. That is to say, the private and public activities of black churches over the course of their history have dealt with the survival of African Americans—the effort to secure resources for African Americans that would allow for their continued existence. To black churches fell "the primary responsibility for the conservation, enhancement, and further development of that unique spiritual quality," writes Wilmore, "that has enabled African and black people of the diaspora to survive and flourish under some of the most unfavorable conditions of the modern world." All is premised on this concern with survival—anything beyond survival assumes it. Survival, then, is the basic impulse of the Black church. And while other approaches that revolve around transformation are part of the religious rhetoric of the Black Church Tradition, the only vision of African American life that has had sustained impact is that of survival, what Wilmore calls the "Survival Tradition."[9] This accounts for the privileging of electoral politics as a way to put in place figures that can satisfy this survival impulse. Reconstruction and the civil rights movement provide two historical markers of electoral politics as essential to the welfare of African Americans, as well as the role (although debatable) of black churches fighting for the rights and obligations associated with this dimension of life in a democracy. Public policy, however, involves a more expansive vision not captured by black churches.

Black churches may serve as the incubator for some skills useful in the public sphere such as communal commitments. However, the resources and theological positions of churches do not allow for the type of information, critical thinking, communication strategies and imaginative approaches to presentation and application of information that mark transformative leadership in the public arena. Private moral values and perspectives might work within the confines of private organizational engagements, but they do not serve the public well, wherein competing claims must be recognized and worked through with respect to and without the rigid boundaries the Black church requires.

To suggest black churches should lead the charge in revitalizing African American communities is to truncate the sources of injustice in the United States that are systemic and tied to a limited application of the principles of democracy. It is to render a private concern, what has been

DOI: 10.1057/9781137376954

in actuality a societal and collective issue. It is to reduce to theologized morality, what is a failure of will to produce the benefits of citizenship. It is to misunderstand the nature of public discourse and to assume it can be ciphered through a spiritualized sense of collective life.

The basic dilemmas facing African Americans are of a socio-political and economic nature and can't be resolved through a myopic sense of culture wars and moral decline. For example, a recent study through the "Economic Mobility Project" clearly indicates that neighborhood poverty, and exposure to poverty, significantly impact the long-term mobility of African American children. Exposure to poverty is a key factor in the gap between the mobility of African Americans and that of white Americans.[10] Poverty also informs other issues such as educational achievement, attitude, and perception of human potential. This is not a cultural issue, and it is not a result of moral fortitude. Rather, it is a matter of economics. "Quality of public amenities like parks and recreation centers, the effectiveness of institutions such as the police, and the degree of exposure to violence, gangs, toxic soil and polluted air," the Economic Mobility Project indicates, "all depend directly on where one lives."[11]

An assumption that African Americans have either slipped away from the old moral standards that once preserved them, or that their moral values in a significant way run contrary to the normative morality of the larger society, are inaccurate and betray more about cultural assumptions than about the actual causes of the socio-economic and political dilemmas currently faced. According to the Pew Research Center ("The Generation Gap and the 2012 Election," 2011), African Americans and white Americans surveyed noted similarities with respect to values, particularly over the past decade. It is more likely the case that generational shifts are marked by greater differences in values and views on morality than noted as a consequence of racial difference. For example, the "Silent Generation" tends to be more conservative on many social issues such as the death penalty and legalization of marijuana than are Millennials, although on abortion rights there is no marked difference. The percentage of African Americans with children out of wedlock is larger, but according to the real numbers, white Americans represent a larger number of United States citizens with children out of wedlock. One might think, "Oh, this is an issue of morality," yet there are economic factors that play into this situation, factors that influence the nature of African American family structure for instance, and that foster a particular set of socio-political challenges.[12] Furthermore, the

DOI: 10.1057/9781137376954

debate concerning the morality of social trauma is not that clear cut, and can't be used to explain the predicament of disadvantaged populations. In fact, the difference is decreasing and almost non-existent between Republican and Democratic perceptions of the moral and ethical climate of the United States (Gallop, "Mood of the Nation" Poll, 2005). However, this is not to say there are no differences in patterns of behavior over against stated morality.

Even if I were to say African Americans are faced with moral challenges, this does not address the causes, nor does it indicate in itself the best means for addressing said challenges. The implicit suggestion that African Americans need to embrace the normative moral code of the larger society does not adequately address the cause of the problem nor does it expose the moral and ethical trauma felt across racial groups. The issue isn't eschewed morality or lack of moral sensibilities. Such thinking continues support for a misguided discussion of pathologies as the proper framework for understanding the nature of African American difficulties. More to the point, it does not validate the assumption by conservatives (and some progressives) that black churches are the central source of transformative public work.

Shared values do not wipe out perceptions of ongoing discrimination faced nor the manner in which economic conditions can dictate life arrangements. Poverty prevents clear thinking in a consistent fashion by forcing a preoccupation with short time frames—"what ifs"—that don't move beyond the immediate needs and don't allow for attention to larger and complex issues. *Rather than quickly turning to morality as the missing link and thereby reducing public obligation, it would be wise and more effective to discern the systemic threats to African American advancement and then address them through public programs and resources distributed and supervised by public institutions creatively arranged and monitored.*

Addressing the problems outlined briefly here is too big a job for the Black church, or any collection of religious institutions for that matter.

The Black church may be able to battle the effects of poverty, for instance, through its theologized perspective on individual value and worth—and in this way have a positive impact on feelings of social (and perhaps political) isolation stemming from the continuing legacy of anti-black racism and its many forms of fall out. This, however, is not to wipe out from African Americans any accountability and responsibility for conduct. Rather, it is to recognize the context for behavior—the

DOI: 10.1057/9781137376954

manner in which economic environments inform and (to some degree) shape life options and perceptions of those options. In a word, morality and socio-economic realities are intertwined. They feed, inform, and justify each other. Any response with a hope of making a difference in the lives of African Americans must be mindful of this and be sophisticated enough and structured in a way to maneuver between the two. This requires a leadership model distinct from what the Black church can provide. *This is not to dismiss black churches, but rather to acknowledge and respect their capacities and limitations and to think about the best way to address the complex challenges facing African Americans in light of this realization.*

On the level of the individual, there may be something to the idea of group identifications (such as with the Black church) impacting what some value and why, how they interact with others, and what they consider of importance about public life. Yet, this does not translate to a public morality. Organizations such as the "High Impact Leadership Coalition" led by Reverend Harry R. Jackson, Jr., of Hope Christian Church (Washington, DC), through its "Black Contract with America on Moral Values," seek to influence and inform debate on moral issues through the lens of biblical teachings. This is a limited approach that circumscribes everything to the cultural world of the Ancient Near East and fails to fully appreciate and account for the links between morality and the contemporary economic condition of African American communities. Morality and socio-political/economic struggles are often blurred; the line between causes and effects becomes fuzzy at best. Yet, one is hard pressed as a matter of evidence rather than politics to indicate a moral failure on the part of African Americans as a cause of negative life conditions. For instance, on issues such as marriage, family, and drug use, there is no clear evidence that African Americans and white Americans differ significantly on the moral implications. Furthermore, there is evidence to suggest urban poverty negatively impacts moral judgment.[13]

Lessons on distinctions between good and evil do little to correct this situation. A matter of inequality at its core, poverty experienced by African Americans requires more than the moralizing of churches.

Even the community programming of churches are fill-gap as opposed to systemic corrections. With this in mind, black churches are best equipped to address localized issues that are responsive to the theologically formed system of moral insights under-girding black church life

DOI: 10.1057/9781137376954

and thought. For instance, addressing the housing needs of church members is within the Black church's domain. The financial resources for such actions, however, should not result from a privileging of church bodies—or religious bodies in general terms—by government. Let churches use their own resources, if these projects are part of their "ministry." Such assistance tends to center on well-positioned, large churches and leave behind average (in size and wealth) black churches. Yet, this is not the basic problem.

More important is the manner in which this funding can blur the line between church and state, damage the secular tone and texture of public conversation and debate, and set-up principles and norms that are narrow and shadowed by the idiosyncrasies of church doctrine.

A surrender of care to religious organizations renders those most in need of assistance vulnerable to the theological whims and parameters of organizations that by their very nature construct a system composed of an "in" group (i.e., those sharing the religious-theological sensibilities of a Christian community) and an "out" group (i.e., those outside the theological and ideological sensibilities of a Christian community)—and the signs of these two groupings is not limited to the most visible symbols of participation in religious activities or explicit use of religious rhetoric.

It is true that religion serves to promote community, but this is community in a limited sense, not the expansive reception of democratic relationships most needed within the workings of the public sphere. Government may attempt to restrict the ability of churches to use funds for explicitly religious activities such as worship, but the natural tendencies of churches is to express allegiance to the faith and to operate programs in light of a missionary or ministerial impulse.

This is a component of the "religious character" of religious organizations, and it is this type of framing of rights and responsibilities that has done deep damage to the workings of our democratic processes. Furthermore, there are ways in which religion tends to polarize, to divide, and this runs contrary to the need for public discourse and actions that unite around a shared agenda for socio-economic and political advancement. Perhaps this reality is one reason 38% of those surveyed in a Pew-sponsored study argue there is too great an expression of faith by political figures. As opposed to 30% indicating that there has been too little, and 25% indicating that the level of faith expressed has been correct.[14] Religion does not provide the proper grammar and

DOI: 10.1057/9781137376954

vocabulary by means of which to conduct public discourse on secular issues such as poverty.

The question isn't whether churches should express their opinions. They should express their social and political opinions consistent with their faith.

However, those opinions and the institutions represent private perspectives that aren't appropriate as frameworks for public policy—and the limited involvement of African American churches in public policy activism up to this point is more appropriate than would be an increase in their participation in public policy and service as a major mechanism of enacting policy decisions.

Personal morality does not make for good public policy. This is not to suggest the public arena is value free. No, instead I am suggesting that the Black church—and religious organizations in more general terms—is too limited ideologically to provide a system of values sufficient to meet the needs of a population extending beyond their membership and immediate communities.

Issues not confined to mid-century understanding of and response to race and racial discrimination are particularly problematic for black churches in that the matrix of morality guiding many of these churches produces a cartography of proper living that is rather reified and drawn from biblical stories without cultural nuance and without the benefit of deep engagement with those not of a similar opinion. No debate, just believe.

By this, I do not intend to privilege "progressive" responses but to simply point out the difficulty churches have on these issues. Church-based notions of morality revolving around perceptions of "sin," combined with limited structures for complex thinking on policy and limited resources, make churches unreliable and a bad choice as the primary advocate for African Americans in the public sphere. What the Black church provides might work within the context of private, individualized morality and values, but it does little to frame public values and morality in a useful and usable way.

What these religious organizations produce are closed worlds monitored and guided by a traditional theological appeal to rightness and evil marked out through moral and ethical codes grounded in a reading of scripture, and requiring consent premised on agreement. That is to say "community" is a contested term within African American Christian thought and practice, and it is not as fluid and flexible as required for

DOI: 10.1057/9781137376954

democratic engagement in the public arena and resolutions to pressing socio-political and economic challenges. As John Green of The Pew Forum on Religion and Public Life, remarks

> It may very well be that the sociability that surrounds religion as real limitations and what it may really be creating is a private-regarding society rather than a public-regarding society. From that point of view, both people on the progressive side who advocate social justice and people on the more traditional side who advocate morality may be on the outs because both of those approaches to religion in public life demand public justice of one kind or another.[15]

Studies suggest most churches are not involved in a heavy or sustained way in public service around large socio-economic issues, and therefore the push for churches to do more related to policy issues and the use of public resources for more expansive programming is external.

To ask churches to provide social services without any attention to the theological positions of those organizations and to believe it can happen in a sustained manner is naive.

Let black churches embrace a prophetic role—offer visions of unified life—but leave the structuring of collective existence in the realms of socio-political and economic developments to organizations better equipped to undertake the task.

Black churches, despite typical narratives regarding the role of black churches, are not equipped to merge the interests of various groups and promote approaches to community advancement that are de-theologized. To clarify my point, my concern is not how particular types of activity in the public sphere—through the securing of governmental resources—might limit the prophetic mission of churches by hampering the ability to critique and challenge. Even prior to developments such as Charitable Choice,[16] the consistent nature and impact of Black church critique and challenge (combined in a form of praxis) has received mixed reviews.

Perhaps the larger issue is more rightly cataloged as the Black church's inherent inability to really impact such issues in a sustained and consistent manner beyond the occasionally elected official or the occasional meeting or protest. The key to addressing the challenges facing African Americans, challenges that are politically and economically derived, is through structures of engagement, robust strategies for communication, and through recognition of the complex systemic strictures to progress. The Black church is ill equipped to provide these.

DOI: 10.1057/9781137376954

To the extent there is a need to work through public morality-related concerns and challenges, it is an issue for the collective. On the level of the individual one might decide to address morality through religious commitment, but on the level of the public there is a need for a more complex and robust moral arrangement. Each person must know two languages of morality, and be comfortable with two ways of moving through the world—one in relationship to private life and the other to public life.

Even if...

I am not arguing that churches have failed to be active. Such a position is difficult to support in that both churches have worked beyond their four walls in both liberal and conservative ways, in light of both "this-worldly" and "other-worldly" orientations.

"Churches," writes sociologist Omar McRoberts, "often pull people together around common ethnicity, regional or national origin, class background, political orientation, life stage, or lifestyle. Less often do congregations form around shared neighborhood identity. Many churches draw membership from a geographic area much wider than the immediate neighborhood."[17] The assumed intimate connection between churches and communities may not be in place and the methods of addressing urban concerns offered by churches could easily be out of step with the actual nature of the issues and the complex needs of the population.

Churches are private organizations unprepared to fully appreciate the nature of the public sphere in that the assumed intimate connection between churches and communities may not be in place and the methods of addressing urban concerns offered by churches could easily be out of step with the actual nature of the issues and the complex needs of the population. For example, black churches have undergone a variety of changes over the past several decades—including some moving out of inner city areas, having a growing population that commutes into the city for church, etc.—that prevent their ability to fully appreciate and respond to the complex needs of city living.

In addition, the very idea of the Black church is an invention of academics like me, and my colleagues. It points to nothing tangible but instead is a "placeholder"—a way of categorizing what is really a range

DOI: 10.1057/9781137376954

of denominations and independent churches that have divergent belief structures, practices, and policies. In fact, the number of denominations and non-denominational churches has increased over the years precisely because of such disagreements. Why, then, should we believe that this system of competing organizations is equipped to undertake the function of public advocate for African Americans, and is the best means by which to address the public plight of African Americans?

Even if churches could be considered a viable and major tool for addressing the public life of African Americans, the structure of the average church would prohibit anything significant. According to sociologist Mark Chaves, only 25% of congregations in the United States have a full-time staff of more than one person.[18] In particular, African American churches lack staff with the training necessary to manage public resources. Equipping churches with the necessary infrastructure would outweigh the benefits of their involvement in public affairs.

It is misguided to assume the ability of churches to meet localized needs such as those covered through the limited construction of housing, or the supply of foodstuff, etc., can equate to the capacity to address the wide-range regional and national issues that shape the public life of African Americans beyond those within a confined geography marked out by church ministry and outreach.

Furthermore, within some black churches, even this ministry to human need is shadowed by a deep suspicion concerning "worldly" matters as having the potential to damage the soul. Hence, "be in the world, but not of the world," as scripture suggest. Yet, is this a proper philosophy of involvement in the secular realm of distribution of public resources and the debate over public policies that affect the lives of African Americans? In addition, serving as an outlet for governmental resource to improve socio-economic conditions also adds another layer of accountability beyond the internal hierarchies established by process within independent congregations or within the context of denominational structures of authority.

Government becomes another source of oversight, with different sensibilities, a different mapping of obligations and different procedures for reporting. This, at best, creates dissonance at the level of accountability and confusion concerning benchmarks for success and time frames. Churches are concerned with mundane markers of improvement, but this is also tied to non-material markers that revolve around the perceived spiritual dimensions of life. The latter should be of no concern within

DOI: 10.1057/9781137376954

the public arena. They produce communities, but in a limited sense—a sense inconsistent with the demands of public policy and distribution of public resources to address major social and economic issues.

There are ways in which black churches have served a lobbyist function for African Americans on the local, state, and national level—seeking to push, as many others do, a particular ideological agenda. One might think of the Jeremiad tradition within African American religious circles—what is considered the prophetic work of the black churches to point out moral failures and to warn against the dire consequences of these failures, if there is no repentance and no correction made. It is one way to think about the social Christianity critique of injustice culminating in the civil rights movement, or the liberation churches guided by black and womanist theologies that outlined the need for radical change in the practices of the United States with respect to black men and women. Yet, why should we give this spiritually fueled lobbying organization control over resources and the public discourse regarding African American life?

Studies indicate that a limited number of churches have secured Charitable Choice funding, and so moving away from this model should not be difficult. Needed are mechanisms for addressing the socio-political and economic needs of African Americans that are not charged in a particular way—do not have another motive or agenda. Churches will have always as an underlying motivation a spiritual dimension, a ministerial ethos brought to bear, and this framing of morality and ethics is too narrow and too restrictive to have any good use within the larger sphere of public effort to apply democratic principles and visions to collective life.

The normative stance of churches by their very nature runs contrary to the best of our democratic vision—it closes off possibilities for the expression of life and liberty when these possibilities should remain expansive and safeguarded. This does not serve as a model for national attention to socio-political and economic problems. Churches are not a substitute for secular, government responsibilities, nor can they replace secular, government-sponsored mechanisms of economic transformation. To put the burden for "redeeming" African American communities, for improving the quality of life for African Americans, on private organizations such as churches hides the problem by individualizing what is actually a systemic issue. And it may also result in a reduction of government accountability and a reduction in public resources used to

DOI: 10.1057/9781137376954

fight issues such as poverty. By taking on this role, then, black churches might unwittingly contribute to the very destruction of communities they claim to value. I am not suggesting black churches should have no form of activism and should express no opinions regarding the activities of the public sphere, rather I am suggesting that private systems such as churches should not dictate public policy and these systems (e.g., churches) should not be used to justify reductions in the meeting of governmental obligations to address public issues of justice and equality.

The public arena should be guided by secularity that recognizes the private merit of religious commitment. But public life demands attention to policy and other matters marked by insights larger than those of a religious tradition.

Notes

1   Quoted in Frederick Harris, *Something Within: Religion in African-American Political Activism* (New York: Oxford University Press, 1999), 97.

2   Quoted in R. Drew Smith and Corwin Smidt, "System Confidence, Congregational Characteristics, and Black Church Civic Engagement," in R. Drew Smith, editor. *New Day Begun: African American Churches and Civic Culture in Post-Civil Rights America* (Durham: Duke University Press, 2003), 60, 62.

3   "A Religious Portrait of African-Americans," January 30, 2009 at: www.pewforum.org/ (page 7 of 14).

4   C. Eric Lincoln and Lawrence H. Mamiya, *The Black Church in the African American Experience* (Durham: Duke University Press, 1990), 201.

5   Mark Chaves, "Religious Congregations," in Lester M. Salamon, editor. *The State of Nonprofit America* (Washington, DC: Brookings Institution Press, 2002), 293.

6   Gary Marx, *Protest and Prejudice: A Study of Belief in the Black Community* (New York: Harper and Row, 1967).

7   "A Religious Portrait of African-Americans," January 30, 2009 at: www.pewforum.org/

8   R. Drew Smith, "Introduction," in R. Drew Smith, *Long March Ahead: African American Churches and Public Policy in Post-Civil Rights America* (Durham: Duke University Press, 2004), 1.

9   Gayraud S. Wilmore, *Black Religion and Black Radicalism: An Interpretation of the Religious History of African Americans*, 3rd edn (Maryknoll, NY: Orbis Books, 1998), 253.

DOI: 10.1057/9781137376954

10 "Neighborhoods and the Black-White Mobility Gap," Economic Mobility Project: An Initiative of The Pew Charitable Trusts.

11 Ibid., 6.

12 Michelle Alexander, *The New Jim Crow* (New York: The New Press, 2011).

13 "Neighborhoods and the Black-White Mobility Gap," Economic Mobility Project: An Initiative of The Pew Charitable Trusts.

14 "More See 'Too Much' Religious Talk by Politicians" at http://www. pewforum.org/Politics-and-Elections

15 "American Grace: How Religion Divides and Unites Us," The Pew Forum on Religion and Public Life, December 16, 2010, at: http://pewforum.org/

16 Charitable Choice involves governmental funding to religious organizations for the purpose of social services. For additional information see, for example, http://georgewbush-whitehouse.archives.gov/government/fbci /guidance/charitable.html. Also see R. Drew Smith, editor, *New Day Begun: African American Churches and Civic Culture in Post-Civil Rights America* (Durham: Duke University Press, 2003), Part III.

17 Omar M. McRoberts, "Black Churches, Community and Development," National Housing Institute, ShelterForce Online (January/February 2001), 3. At: http://www.nhi.org/online/issues/115/McRoberts.html

18 Chaves, "Religious Congregations," in Salamon, *State of Nonprofit America*, 276.

DOI: 10.1057/9781137376954

5
Testing My Claim: A Response to Religious Progressives

Abstract: *In this chapter, I use an email exchange with Rabbi Michael Lerner as a way of further exploring the potential and limitations of theism as the language for public discourse. While acknowledging what theism attempts to offer public discourse, I argue there are limitations concerning language and vision that hamper what theism can help achieve. Instead, I push for collaboration and cooperation in a way that calls for new mechanisms and structures for public engagement.*

Pinn, Anthony B. *What Has the Black Church to Do with Public Life?* New York: Palgrave Macmillan, 2013.
DOI: 10.1057/9781137376954.

DOI: 10.1057/9781137376954

My thinking in the previous chapters spilled over into a few email exchanges that merit some consideration. Rabbi Michael Lerner, in an email, raised interesting questions concerning my thinking on the relationship of theism to public issues.

He, as a theist, and I, as a non-theistic humanist, do not share a perspective on the topic. As I expressed to Rabbi Lerner, I am troubled by and push against reliance on theistic organizations to shape the values and agenda of public discourse. I know my non-theist colleagues would agree with me. However, the issue isn't so easily resolved. In fact, a brief exchange with Rabbi Lerner sparked follow-up questions (in italics) that deserve a thoughtful response—and I want to understand the following as the beginning of such a response.

There is some overlap with ideas presented in the previous chapters, but the context of Rabbi Lerner's questions makes that information important to maintain. Keeping some overlap in place also brings to the fore some of the non-theistic humanist inclinations informing much of my concern and critique.[1]

Finally, including this chapter is also meant to suggest an invitation for exchange, for debate over my critique and my suggestions.

▶ *The Black church has been the major means by which African Americans have been mobilized to engage the public sphere. What institution can replace it, and doesn't your strategy aid the conservative right and the religious right by silencing the primary source of political activism in African American communities?*

It is often the case that the quality and quantity of church involvement in civil rights political activity is over-stated. Many were inactive, and some African American Christians were activists despite their churches. For example, a study of the Birmingham movement indicates that 400 churches did not support the movement over against 60 churches that participated by holding meetings.[2] Whether churches participated or not in collective action, many of them had in place more modest structures for meeting localized needs.

Along these lines, I applaud and encourage churches to use resources to provide "real time" assistance through soup kitchens, shelters, and so on. But this action and the theological language used to describe this ethical commitment do not translate into a framework for public engagement that can cut across all the various modalities of personal life stances. Furthermore, I am not the first to make this particular argument,

DOI: 10.1057/9781137376954

so I simply provide my spin (as a theologian and humanist scholar) on what numerous scholars have argued: the very organizational structure of churches entails hierarchial authority in a way that does not foster a sense of inclusion, and does not correspond to the type of robust and varied public sphere in which the best thinking, speaking, and acting take place.[3]

The insider/outsider dichotomy at work within church organizational structure is premised on a theological justification that isn't subject to traditional rules of evidence and counter argument. Instead, cosmic authorities are appealed to and, for the members of these organizations, such authorities overrule mundane authorities. While this might work for the interior life of these organizations, it doesn't provide a useful framing of public exchange.

As important as a realistic assessment of church activism over the past several decades is realistic attention to a faulty ideology guiding ongoing assumptions concerning the public importance of theistic organizations. In short, the assumption of church involvement as essential to progressive activism is based on a fallacy. Religious organizations such as black churches are not the only means by which citizens are able to address their collective (and private) lives. "The idea," Eddie Glaude notes, "of this venerable institution as central to black life and as a repository for the social and moral conscience of the nation has all but disappeared."[4] Glaude shares this as part of a call for conversation, as an opportunity to think through and reconfigure the nature and meaning of black churches in African American life. I, however, have something different in mind—a push beyond any assumption that theistic organizations can or should play a substantive role in public life.

I am not arguing against church progressive activism, but rather I am noting the natural limitations of and context for this religious encounter with human need. Recent studies suggest a decrease in black church activism, and this may not be a bad thing, but rather an opportunity to assess and determine new strategies, a more robust and expansive language for public discourse, and new mechanisms of delivery. As R. Drew Smith notes, church activism hit its high mark during the 1950s and 1960s, but has declined since then.[5] The inability to agree on "an African American public policy agenda" is a contributing factor, but it also makes sense to question the very ability of theistic vocabulary to frame public conversation about even shared objectives. There is, as Smith acknowledges, increasing "social and political diversity" that challenges churches'

DOI: 10.1057/9781137376954

ability to define the terms of public engagement. It is also the case that black churches, while active at times on public policy related issues, have by and large limited their most substantial attention to civil rights and socio-economic concerns focused on the US.[6]

While public debate must include a variety of opinions and perspectives, public exchange at its best requires maintenance of expansive possibilities. And there are numerous examples of an inability of churches to play by these rules. Churches are marked by theological conservatism that often hampers progressive activism. For example, one need only think of the ministers who suggested African Americans should avoid voting until they've had a chance to meet with President Obama concerning his stance on gay marriage.[7] Some ministers also critiqued the NAACP for its affirming stance on gay marriage.[8] These are not exceptions, nor do they represent a marginal conservatism. These ministers, while more vocal than most, represent a common retrograde, a conservative ethos in conflict with the liberal posture of churches on certain other race-based issues. Furthermore, the theological limitations on what churches perceive as "healthy" families as well as the general discomfort with physical bodies means churches are not the best arbiters of public policy related to physical health and families.

Beyond issues related to marriage and family, framings of relationship to the natural environment as "stewardship" does not necessarily promote the best understandings of environmental policy in that it can maintain a distance between humans and the rest of the natural environment, a distance that can allow for policies lacking sensitivity to more than human desire for growth and expansion. Stewardship can often mean for church members and leaders responsible use as opposed to interconnectedness and dependence. While this problematic thinking regarding relationship between humans and the rest of the natural environment clearly exists outside churches, only theistic organizations can invest this with divine sanction in a way that makes challenge to it difficult.

> ▸ *Doesn't the history of the SCLC and Dr. King in particular suggest a way to overcome the "bad" theology—framing a defeatist sense of moral evil—through their appeal to "action oriented" theological themes in the scriptures? Why not simply revive that tradition?*

My objection does not involve challenge to a "defeatist sense of moral evil." Mine is not an argument over theological support for activism or passivity. I acknowledge the existence of a theological tradition

DOI: 10.1057/9781137376954

supporting engagement articulated in the Social Gospel and then various forms of liberation theology. Mindful of this tradition and Rabbi Lerner's question, I suggest the theological language and content of church activism actually involves a certain triumphantalism, guided by a teleological sense of history and a posture of manifest destiny. It is action oriented, but premised on a bad logic—a warped economy of moral evil. That is to say, this hopefulness in the face of moral evil is oddly premised on one's absorption of moral evil as having some type of redemptive quality (when, in the case of Dr. King, it is undeserved). In the words of so many black Christians, "no cross, no crown."[9] And, whether this theological platform is labeled conservative or liberal, these theological options easily fall victim to this redemptive suffering model of engagement, and there are dire consequences to this line of theological thinking.

Even if this thinking is flexible enough to allow for periodic engagement with public issues, it does not promote the type of posture toward public issues that allows for full critique and address of the challenges impacting quality of life because there remains a perception that good comes out of moral evil on the collective level. Furthermore, even this good is premised on the workings of a God thereby rendering engagement of public issues a theistic enterprise. As a consequence, the work of the civil rights movement involved an effort to do good work despite a redemptive suffering perception of moral evil. This theological perspective on moral evil has remained the "gold" standard within church circles, promoting a theological conservativism with a flexible political conservative/liberal binary.[10] Hence, the challenge isn't to go back to some romanticized sense of theological correctness housed in the strategies of the civil rights movement's primary organization; rather, the challenge is to leave behind redemptive suffering models and to refine public discourse.

Isn't it possible that this economy of moral evil promoted by redemptive suffering arguments resulted in a theological justification almost akin to that used for slavery? In both instances, those with power are able to point to their role (as problematic as it might be) as an indispensable component of the cosmic plan: with respect to slavery, because the story of Ham, etc., points to divine intent carried out by slaveholders; and, for the latter, if the "crown" requires the "cross," socio-political and economic trauma are the necessary "trial" by fire.

DOI: 10.1057/9781137376954

▶ *Leading figures such as Rabbi Michael Lerner have provided compelling arguments for a new form of progressive-religious activism that draws from the theme of the "Left Hand of God." Why not work to increase the presence of this perspective in the public arena to the extent it has the capacity to include all and doesn't require a particular religious path?*

This re-evaluation of the proper tone and content of public discourse and the organizations used to arrange sources in light of that discourse should take into consideration the human quest for meaning—for life meaning; but it is a mistake to assume the language of spirituality or more narrowly religiosity captures "meaning." Spirituality and religiosity are too restrictive in that this desire for meaning has to do with a general yearning for continuity, for relationships, and for purpose that explodes the limited framing associated with even the most expansive sense of the religious. It doesn't capture my sense of the quest for life meaning, and it doesn't capture this sense of life meaning for other non-theists like me. As hard as he tries, and his efforts are noteworthy, even the *Left Hand of God* approach promoted by Rabbi Lerner does not capture those outside a framing of meaning dependent on some form of the supernatural.

The conceptual organization offered by the "Left Hand of God," meant to counter the religious and political right seems to simply draw from the other side of theism—a more progressive theism, but theism nonetheless. There is a crisis of meaning, on this Rabbi Lerner and I agree. And, it is manifest in the particular modes of materialism and the devaluation of human bodies and minds—the layered xenophobia—associated with them. However, to frame this crisis as a spiritual crisis is too myopic and it truncates what is rather a complex arrangement of dissatisfying relationships of which religion is often a component.

Rabbi Lerner's framing longs to include a full range of citizens— theists and atheists—but the language is restrictive. What this framing may provide is an opportunity for theists of various orientations to seek common ground not hampered by differing beliefs, and in this way it might provide a private rationale for their public interests, but it does not serve as the conceptual underpinning for a public discourse and policies that cut across the tensions of theism and non-theism. Hence, it cannot serve as the basis for public discourse leading to public policy and the implementation of these policies.

DOI: 10.1057/9781137376954

Individuals are complex and exist simultaneously in multiple spaces of life meaning including (for some) spaces of religious identity, and they are not disconnected from these various identities when participating in public life. However, this does not mean one of these narrow identities—religious identity and beliefs—can serve as the bridge identity for the public arena. Such a move does not free us from the possibility of poor judgment and oppressive behavior—on this Rabbi Lerner is correct. Yet, what this move away from religious framing of transformative efforts does promote is the opportunity to address these shortcomings without cosmic justifications and scriptural arguments that do not easily bend to the will of logic and historical evidence.

Such a position does not of necessity collapse into nihilism, nor is it defeatist and shortsighted with respect to the gains made and the bright spots in our collective history. Rather it involves measured realism—the deep recognition of both our collective good and our collective misdeeds as a synergy of experience, an already and always connected framing of life. This is not a surrender of our future to only what we believe can be achieved easily.

No, measured realism maintains a desire for robust and complex life, but is ever mindful of our flaws and the real chance we may not live out our dreams. Not floored by this, measured realism then pushes its adherents to actually value our struggle for life filled with meaning. This is not a call for redemptive suffering notions of progress, but rather to be mindful of the real possibility we may never reach our desired outcomes—but we struggle for those outcomes nonetheless. Such an environment of struggle isn't value free—yet why assume only theism/religion can promote a set of values worthy of allegiance? Rabbi Lerner calls for a reframing of love—"love of money needs to be replaced by love of life, love of the earth, love of God, and love of each other at the center of our economic lives."[11] The values communicated by Rabbi Lerner with such great passion are rendered inseparable from their theistic base, and as a result they do become deeply connected with theism through the symbol of the Left Hand of *God*. We non-theistic humanists (and there are many of us) are not captured in this framing of life's web of relationship. Why assume the stories of our lives are best read through the hermeneutics of theistic, sacred texts, or best harnessed by appeal to a cosmic "other"?

The very inclusion of "God" and the assumption of ethical action as drawn from religious texts may seem minor to theists, but it is a major

DOI: 10.1057/9781137376954

sign of exclusion for non-theists. Thinking about what Rabbi Lerner suggests from the perspective of a non-theistic humanist sheds some light on the problem with theological language as normative language. And, this non-theistic perspective views "God" as a signifier, a sign meant to motivate certain postures toward self, others, and the world. Thinking about this as a process of naming meant to capture certain values, desires, and motivations, God, in crude terms, is the "intangible asset" that brands numerous forms of theism—that drives that brand of meaning making.[12] But it isn't universally recognized. It doesn't stimulate in all who hear it the type of commitment meant and value formation necessary in the public arena of ideas and action. That space requires a language that motivates us to our better selves. Reaction to this example may just highlight the gulf between theists and non-theists on the ability of this particular signifier to harness and push our best imaginings.

How does a non-theist read herself into this progressive movement in light of claims such as this: "What the Left needs is an alternative view of who God is, not a denial of God and religion"?[13] It comes across as if non-theists are invited to participate in this particular vision of meaning making as public activity, if they are willing to leave at home their disbelief. What of the growing number of "Nones" within the United States? How are they represented by this particular take on the sociopolitical and economic necessity of God? Perhaps what we need as the basis of public discourse and as grounding for public policy is a *healthy life-centered* vision of life as opposed to a religious one?

At times Rabbi Lerner seems to qualify appeal to divinity or God:

> The fact is that human beings cannot live happily without a framework of meaning that transcends the individualism, materialism, and selfishness of the marketplace and without the sense that a loving connection exists among us as well as to *that larger experience the religious among us call God.* (Italics added)[14]

This posture may (hopefully) damage the claims of the religious right to the public arena; yet, like the religious right, this progressive perspective assumes the normativity of theistic vocabulary as public vocabulary. Such an approach as that offered by Rabbi Lerner provides a worthwhile challenge to theists with respect to the deep dimensions of human life, human be-*ing*, that inform private and public interactions. Yet, its grammar (and resulting framing of ethics) does not extend beyond a theistic

DOI: 10.1057/9781137376954

life orientation and the source materials for this theism. The public arena must be guided by rules of engagement and framed by a vocabulary of exchange more human and less theistic than this.

If humanists have been too quick to label all religious persons as fundamentalists and attack on this level, theists have been too quick to presume they could capture all the nuance of humanism through a quick dismissal of "New Atheism."

Everyone, as Rabbi Lerner passionately calls for, should be invited to participate in the public life of the United States; however, I simply seek to qualify this with the argument that such involvement entails being bilingual—one's personal "faith" stance and its vocabulary, but also a public language based on values not confined to or by theism— but more deeply connected to a broad concern for life and forged through the best vocabulary of democratic ideals. This process is about life meaning—and it cannot be articulated using the language of one particular frame of meaning making called religion. Values sufficient for the public arena must be shaped and communicated by a language expansive enough to carry the full weight of a fantastic standard of life. Developing this alternate language of public life might, for example, require sustained conversation between theists and humanist organizations such as the American Humanist Association that extends beyond mutual critique to collaborative strategies for improving the conditions of life for all. And, buttressing these conversations there would be a central question: what are the terms and content of a language robust enough to capture this vision across ideological and (a)theological lines? What is the basic, and shared, ethical considerations motivated by this new public language?

New language, robust values, new structures of delivery, and mechanisms of accountability beyond the narrow claims of any one community are needed. This alone will allow for substantive work toward a transformed world built by means of human ingenuity and creativity—and premised on a healthy respect for the private faith orientations of all.

We need new processes for delivery, new approaches to use of public resources, and clear thinking on the true nature of impoverished life. Anything short of systemic alterations, the use of public resources through organizations and programs not beholden to particular theological positions, is to put a bandage on a gaping wound. Yet, this strategy is at times entertained by political figures. As Megan McLaughlin notes, conversation concerning civil society has involved a spectrum of opinion

DOI: 10.1057/9781137376954

related to public support—with some wanting governmental support for programs, etc., meant to alleviate poverty and other forms of inequality. Others understand civil society rhetoric as affording an opportunity to shift responsibility for community issues to individuals and private organizations such as churches. Tied to the latter is at times an implicit assumption that government should remain outside such intervention because poverty and other issues are the consequence of poor morals and values; and, these are best handled by religious organizations and the like.[15] The Personal Responsibility and Work Opportunity Reconciliation Act of 1996 (PRWORA), while pushing responsibility away from federal government to the state, McLaughlin reflects, played into the assumption that private organizations such as churches should take the lead in addressing issues of poverty. Some who support this are well-intentioned, but it is an approach that does little good.[16]

We should take seriously calls for creative thinking and aggressive strategies, but rather than trying to retro-fit theistic organizations based on the assumed glory of their past, it's time to develop new organizations, and a new language of public engagement to meet current needs for transformed living.

Notes

1 These questions are drawn from an email exchange with Rabbi Michael Lerner.

2 Kraig Byerlein and Kenneth T. Andrews, "Black Voting During the Civil Rights Movement: A Micro-Level Analysis," *Social Forces*, Volume 87, Number 1 (September 2008): 8.

3 See for example, Adolph Reed, *The Jesse Jackson Phenomenon: The Crisis of Purpose in Afro-American Politics* (New Haven: Yale University Press, 1986), chapter 5 in particular.

4 Eddie Glaude, "The Black Church Is Dead," *Huffington Post*, 2/24/10.

5 R. Drew Smith, *Long March Ahead: African American Churches and Public Policy in Post-Civil Rights America* (Durham: Duke University Press, 2004), 9.

6 Ibid., 11–14.

7 http://www.christianpost.com/news/black-pastors-lay-down-gauntlet-to-obama-over-same-sex-marriage-77596/

8 http://www.catholicnewsagency.com/news/african-american-leaders-blast-naacp-gay-marriage-support/

DOI: 10.1057/9781137376954

9   Anthony B. Pinn, *Why, Lord? Suffering and Evil in Black Theology* (New York: Continuum), 1995.

10 Anthony B. Pinn, *Moral Evil and Redemptive Suffering* (Gainesville, FL: University Press of Florida), 2001.

11 Michael Lerner, *The Left Hand of God: Taking Back Our Country from the Religious Right* (New York: HarperSanFransciso, 2006), 234.

12 This language and the inspiration for attention to the significance of branding and name came from reading John Colapinto, "Famous Names," *The New Yorker* (October 3, 2011, 38–43. The phrase "intangible asset" is drawn from Keven Lane Keller, quoted on page 39 of the article, and here it is applied to the linguistic arrangement of theological meaning.

13 Lerner, *The Left Hand of God*, 99.

14 Ibid., 65.

15 Megan McLaughlin, "The Role of African American Churches in Crafting the 1996 Welfare Reform Policy," in Smith, *Long March Ahead*, 53.

16 Ibid.

DOI: 10.1057/9781137376954

6
Restating the Claim

Abstract: *This chapter is the conclusion for the volume in which I reiterate the limitations of theism within the public arena, and call for new structures and organizations for engagement with public concerns and issues.*

Pinn, Anthony B. *What Has the Black Church to Do with Public Life?* New York: Palgrave Macmillan, 2013.
DOI: 10.1057/9781137376954.

This volume is a manifesto—a stating of my opinion—on what I consider a vital topic. It is not a condemnation of black churches and other theistic organizations; it is not an effort to render them invisible. Rather, it is a repositioning of them in light of their infrastructure and capacities.

Despite a long history of effort to participate in (if not shape or determine) public life, I see little in the way of long-lasting developments that are dependent on the unique resources of these churches and others like them. And while these churches may have value on the level of the individual, and I have no major problem with theism as personal source of life meaning, they have limited utility within the public arena.

Simply because churches have been involved in public life doesn't mean they should remain involved; it doesn't mean their involvement has been necessary or ultimately useful. To the contrary, the theological framework of these churches limits their capacity with regard to public discourse. Their organizational and managerial structure privilege unchecked "calling" and is based on creedal formulations that inhibit participation on issues of public life and public policy that run contrary to the narrow scope of churches and church leadership.

Churches work based on knowledge sets that require faith as opposed to rigorous debate and evidence that should mark public exchange on vital issues. Even efforts to work beyond the most visible limitations of religious organizations, like those of Rabbi Lerner, ultimately produce a narrowness of vision based on the limitations of theistic criteria for activism.

Bravo for black churches and other organizations to the extent they limit themselves to the private dimensions of life. I say this despite my personal concern with moving beyond theism. Yet, I say it in that I don't see human progress as demanding the end of religion, but rather we must have real limits on the public harm religious organizations—their teachings and practices—produce.

I suggest beginning this work of limiting harm with full recognition of the inappropriate nature of religious organizations within the public arena. Religious people yes, but religion in the public arena, no.

Perhaps the decrease in the number of US citizens who claim religion, as well as the decrease in the percentage of citizens (believers and others) who see it as having significant influence on life speaks to the need for the type of considerations I have proposed here. Religious people tend to believe that a more religious citizenry would benefit the

DOI: 10.1057/9781137376954

nation. This is to be expected. Yet, oddly enough even those who attend religious gatherings less often also see religion as having a potentially beneficial impact on life. But based on the failures of religious organizations regarding pressing social issues and the inconsistencies of religious leaders, this point of view could simply be code for a longing for citizens who have more rigorous moral and ethical platforms for individual and collective life. This, of course, is speculation on my part. However, if nothing else, changing perspectives on the nature and function of religion as evidenced by Gallop polls and Pew Foundation studies speak to the need to reconsider the role of religion in the public arena.[1] As I believe these studies and surveys suggest, people can maintain a personal commitment to religion (however it is defined) and see it as having limited impact on public life. I suggest, however, this isn't a situation to be lamented, but rather one to be encouraged: be religious in private life, but committed to a public arena guided by fewer narrow and theologically fixed perceptions and visions of collective well-being.

I make this distinction recognizing that people are as they are with respect to religion, and this commitment to religion will impact their private lives. However, what I call for is a bilingual framework whereby people are free to use their religious language within the context of their private lives, but participation in the public arena, on issues of policy, etc., requires use of a different language because this arena need be secular.

This is *not* to suggest an anti-religious state, but instead a public arena neutral regarding the "truth" of religion or of atheism. It is a form of collective life based upon arguments that can be verified, and perspectives that privilege the integrity of life in broad and robust ways beyond artificial confinements and restrictions demanded by theistic creeds and doctrines.

No doubt many will disagree with my perspective and my characterization of the Black church in particular and theism in general. I didn't write this anticipating full agreement with my views and opinions.

I write at the end of this book what I wrote at the beginning—this is a call for conversation. It is a call for creative and innovative approaches to the transformation of our collective, public life while being mindful of where theism fits and doesn't fit into this process. This slim volume outlines my take on this topic. What is yours?

DOI: 10.1057/9781137376954

Note

1   I make these various comments in response to two fairly recent sets of findings. See "Most Americans Say Religion Is Losing Influence in U.S.," May 29, 2013 (http://www.gallupc.om/poll/162803/americans-say-religion-losing-influence.aspx. Also see: " 'Nones' on the Rise: One-in-Five Adults Have No Religious Affiliation," October 9, 2012, Pew Research Center, The Pew Forum on Religion and Public Life (http://www.pewforum.org /Unaffiliated/nones-on-the-rise.aspx).

DOI: 10.1057/9781137376954

Selected Bibliography

Alexander, Michelle. *The New Jim Crow* (New York: The New Press, 2011).

Blassingame, John W., editor. *Slave Testimony: Two Centuries of Letters, Speeches, Interviews, and Autobiographies* (Baton Rouge: Louisiana State University Press, 1977).

Byerlein, Kraig and Kenneth T. Andrews, "Black Voting During the Civil Rights Movement: A Micro-Level Analysis," *Social Forces*, Volume 87, Number 1 (September 2008), 65–93.

Cone, James H. *For My People: Black Theology and the Black Church* (Maryknoll, NY: Orbis Books, 1984).

Franklin, John Hope. *From Slavery to Freedom: A History of Negro Americans*, 5th edn (New York: Alfred A. Knopf, 1980).

George, Carol V. R., *Segregated Sabbaths: Richard Allen and the Rise of Independent Black Churches, 1760–1840* (New York: Oxford University Press, 1973).

Giggie, John M. *After Redemption: Jim Crow and the Transformation of African American Religion in the Delta, 1875–1915* (New York: Oxford University Press, 2008).

Harris, Frederick. *Something Within: Religion in African-American Political Activism* (New York: Oxford University Press, 1999).

Harvey, Paul. *Freedom's Coming: Religious Culture and the Shaping of the South from the Civil War through the Civil Rights Era* (Chapel Hill: University of North Carolina, 2008).

Lerner, Michael. *The Left Hand of God: Taking Back Our Country from the Religious Right*, rev updated edn (New York: HarperOne, 2007).

Lincoln, C. Eric and Lawrence H. Mamiya, *The Black Church in the African American Experience* (Durham: Duke University Press, 1990).

Marable, Manning. *How Capitalism Underdeveloped Black America* (Boston: South End Press, 1983).

Montgomery, William E. *Under Their Own Vine and Fig Tree: The African-American Church in the South, 1865–1900* (Baton Rouge: Louisiana State University).

Moses, Wilson Jeremiah, *Black Messiahs and Uncle Toms: Social and Literary Manipulations of a Religious Myth* (University Park: The Pennsylvania State University Press, 1982).

Paris, Peter. *The Social Teaching of the Black Churches* (Philadelphia: Fortress Press, 1985).

Pinn, Anthony B. *The Black Church in the Post-Civil Rights Era* (Maryknoll, NY: Orbis Books, 2002).

Pinn, Anthony B., editor. *Moral Evil and Redemptive Suffering* (Gainesville, FL: University Press of Florida, 2001).

Pinn, Anthony B., editor. *Making the Gospel Plain: The Writings of Bishop Reverdy C. Ransom* (Harrisburg: Trinity Press International, 1999).

Pinn, Anthony B. *Why, Lord? Suffering and Evil in Black Theology* (New York: Continuum, 1995).

Raboteau, Albert. *Slave Religion: The "Invisible Institution" in the Antebellum South* (New York: Oxford University Press, 1978).

Salamon, Lester M., editor. *The State of Nonprofit America* (Washington, DC: Brookings Institution Press, 2002).

Sernett, Milton C. *Bound for the Promised Land: African American Religion and the Great Migration* (Durham: Duke University Press, 1997).

Smith, R. Drew, ed. *Long March Ahead: African American Churches and Public Policy in Post-Civil Rights America* (Durham: Duke University Press, 2004).

Smith, R. Drew, ed. *New Day Begun: African American Churches and Civic Culture in Post-Civil Rights America* (Durham: Duke University Press, 2003).

Wilmore, Gayraud S. *Black Religion and Black Radicalism: An Interpretation of the Religious History of African Americans*, 3rd edn (Maryknoll, NY: Orbis, 1998).

DOI: 10.1057/9781137376954

Index

DOI: 10.1057/9781137376954

DOI: 10.1057/9781137376954

CPSIA information can be obtained at www.ICGtesting.com
Printed in the USA
LVOW08*2209290813

350293LV00005B/34/P